The Official Centenary History

ONE HUNDRED YEARS OF

GOODISON GLORY

The Official Centenary History

ONE HUNDRED YEARS OF GOODISON GLORY

by Ken Rogers

BREEDON
BOOKS
SPORT

First published in Great Britain by
The Breedon Books Publishing Company Limited
44 Friar Gate, Derby DE1 1DA
1992

ISBN 1 873626 11 8

Printed and bound in Great Britain by The Bath Press Limited, Bath.
Jacket printed by BDC Printing Services Ltd of Derby.

Contents

In The Footsteps Of The Greats 6

The Finest And Most Complete Ground
    In The Whole Kingdom 7

Introduction 9

George Mahon's Dream — And The
    'Kicking' Of King John 11

Laughter, Hisses, Uproar — And A New
    Home! 18

The Terms of Settlement — And On To
    Goodison .19

A Ground Fit For Kings and Queens   21

Minutes Leading To Golden Hours —
    And The Naming Of Goodison
    Park 23

Training For The High Standard Of
    Efficiency .26

Hail Goodison, Hail Everton! 29

First League Victory At Goodison 31

Southworth's Record Six-Goal Blitz . . .33

Houlding Kicked Again — In The First
    'Derby' 35

Shouts, Shrieks, Groans, Cheers — And
    Then Handshakes All Round! 38

The Goodison Turnstile Fraud of 1895 42

The Goodison Park Riot 44

Everton's Biggest Ever First Division
    Victory 45

Last Gasp Champions On A Day Of
    High Drama 49

Ten Thousand Holes In Blackburn
    Lancashire's Defence! 52

Dixie Signs In For A Goal-den Future 55

Dean's First Goodison Treble 57

A Goodison Christmas Cracker 58

One Down, Fifty-Nine To Go 61

Dixie Dean's Finest Hour 63

Sagar Begins His Goodison Marathon   69

Relegated After A Storming Victory!   70

A Whole New Second Division
    Experience 72

Seven Goals Before Half-Time 74

Promoted At The First Attempt 78

Twelve goals At Goodison In One Day 79

Hail To Sunshine Dixie! 81

The Old One-Two . . .Champs At The
    Double 83

Goodison's Greatest Ever Cup Tie? . . .86

The Master And The Pupil 89

Dixie's Heading Out! 91

Dixie Has His 60 Goals — Gordon His
    60 Years! .93

Champions — And Then It's War 98

Bring In The Crowds — 78,299 Of
    Them! 102

England's First Home Defeat Against
    Foreign Rivals 106

That Sinking Feeling 109

Blood And Thunder Cup Triumph   114

Heading Back To The Big Time 120

Lighting Up Goodison Park 125

Carey Takes A Taxi Ride — And The
    'Millionaires' Take Centre Stage   128

Vernon Makes It V-Day 138

Milan Maestros Hit Town 145

World-Class Memories Of Pelé, Eusebio
    and Gallant North Korea 156

The Ultimate Trophy Parade 163

Champions — And Entertainers 173

Germans Crushed In Penalty Shoot-Out 178

Latchford's £10,000 Jackpot 188

Happiness . . .Crushing Manchester
    United 197

The Pride of Germany Blitzed 199

We Shall Not Be Moved 203

Record-Breaking Champions 207

Lineker's Goodison Swansong 210

Two Title Trophies In One Day! 214

The Match Of A Lifetime 217

Gwladys Street's Last Stand 222

Enter Peter Beardsley — The Geordie
    Genius 225

Servants of Everton 228

Bibliography .237

Subscribers 238

In The Footsteps Of The Greats

COMPILING this history of Good-ison Park has obviously involved considerable research and months of work behind a typewriter, but it was not so much a chore as pleasure. My father lifted me over the Goodison turnstiles as a toddler (that's sixpence I owe the club!) to watch my first Everton game as a new decade dawned at the start of the 1950s.

I went to Major Lester School in Everton Valley and played all of my early football in Stanley Park, the original home of St Domingo FC and then Everton. Perhaps it was inevitable that I would follow the fortunes of the Blues. Incredibly, while I was immersed in the final stages of completing this Centenary History of Goodison, I found myself playing on the famous pitch for the very first time, at the age of 43.

As I said to one of my teammates in a 'businessmen's game' prior to Andy King's benefit match: "Magnificent — but 25 years too late!"

Perhaps it was because my head was full of names like Edgar Chadwick, Jack Southworth, Sandy Young, Harry Makepeace, Dixie Dean, Tommy Law-ton and the rest, that the experience was extra-special. It was a wonderful feeling to be treading in the footsteps of the greats. And I even scored a penalty at the Gwladys Street End that Roy Vernon himself would have been proud of.

I would like to thank Andy King for making that possible and attempt to thank one or two other people now for their invaluable co-operation. Colin Hunt, Les Rawlinson, Geoff Churney and the other members of the 'Liverpool Daily Post & Echo' Library team gave tremendous support on the photographic side. Everton's chief executive Jim Greenwood and commercial manager Derek Johnston were always a source of encouragement and I thank Howard Kendall for his interest and his knowledge.

My former 'Liverpool Echo' colleague Harold Wolfe, whose journalist father John was one of the respected early members of the Goodison Park press box, provided much valuable information. George Higham's enthusiasm and help is also noted, likewise the valuable assistance of Rob Porter and noted Merseyside historian Derek Whale. My appreciation goes to everybody who had an in-put into this publication, and that means all the writers and reporters who chronicle football, week in, week out, effectively compiling match reports, but in real terms writing the history books of tomorrow. Here's to the next hundred years at Goodison Park.

The Finest And Most Complete Ground In The Whole Kingdom

*B*EHOLD *Goodison Park! No single picture could take in the entire scene the ground presents, it is so magnificently large, for it rivals the greater American baseball pitches. On three sides of the field of play there are tall covered stands, and on the fourth side the ground has been so well banked up with thousands of loads of cinders that a complete view of the game can be held from any position.*

The spectators are divided from the playing piece by a neat, low hoarding, and the touchline is far enough from it to prevent those accidents which used to be predicted at Anfield Road, but never happened. Taking it altogether, it appears to be one of the finest and most complete grounds in the whole kingdom, and it is to be hoped that the public will liberally support the promoters.

'Out of Doors' publication
October 1892.

Behold Goodison Park! After 100 years it remains a breathtaking spectacle, a venue steeped in history and tradition.

It rivals just about any soccer stronghold in the land, surrounded on three sides by towering all-seater stands. The fourth side, perhaps the only section of the ground a time traveller from the past might recognise, contains the one remaining standing area, a strip of terracing at the Stanley Park End beneath a den of seats occupied by visiting hordes these days.

The triple-decker Main Stand on Goodison Road soars majestically into a royal blue sky and those venturing into its Top Balcony enjoy a bird's-eye view of one of the lushest playing surfaces in Britain.

Taking it altogether, it IS one of the finest and most complete grounds in the kingdom, an arena fit for Champions.

Ken Rogers
September 1992

This is possibly the first image of Goodison Park, a very rough sketch of 'the new Everton football ground' – published in the 'Liverpool Football Echo' on 13 August 1892. It is clearly not to scale with the palings on the right (the Goodison Road side) too close to the pitch. A cinder bank sloped back on this side. But is nevertheless a fascinating insight into England's first major football stadium.

Goodison Park in November 1892, when the Blues entertained Heart of Midlothian. This drawing was published in the 'Outdoors Magazine'. The original church of St Luke the Evangelist is clearly visible. This was a temporary structure that was eventually re-sited in Blowick, near Southport, making way for the present church in 1901.

Goodison Park as it looked from 1938 when the Gwladys Street Stand was completed in time for a Royal visit. The stadium then changed very little until 1971 when the magnificent 1909 Main Stand made way for today's equally magnificent structure.

How an artist envisaged the breathtaking triple-decker Main Stand that was finally completed in 1971.

Introduction

GOODISON Park is 100 years old. This book is a celebration of this very special football landmark. It does not aspire to be the definitive history of Everton Football Club. The birth of the Blues has already been dealt with in previous publications, not least in the 'History of Everton 1878-1929' by Thomas Keates and the 'Official Centenary History' by John Roberts, published in 1978.

The aim of this latest offering, commissioned by the club, is to highlight the glory years associated with one of the most famous and historic grounds in the world, a venue that has entertained kings and queens, hosted FA Cup Finals, staged major World Cup matches and been the scene of a thousand and one dramatic Football League battles.

Goodison Park is the home of football legends and the eventful careers and feats of many of those giants of yesteryear are captured in words and pictures on these pages. The author makes no apology for repeating the story of the famous 'split' that inspired Everton to leave Anfield and cross Stanley Park for pastures new. No book about Goodison would be complete without a clear assessment of the arguments and counter-arguments leading to the club's historic change of venue. It was a decision that led to the formation of Liverpool Football Club and the beginning of a rivalry that continues to amaze outsiders and inspire locals, a blue and red battle of wits that constantly fires the imagination.

Further research has revealed a host of new angles. The hand-written club 'minute' books of 1892, gathering dust in the Goodison vault, bring alive the characters and pioneers of the last century who were brave enough to plot a new beginning. This book salutes their initiative. It also gives a fascinating insight into the training methods of the last century and compares them with late 20th-century requirements. There is an insight into the Goodison Park turnstile frauds of 1895 and the Goodison Park Riot which took place the same year.

But the main body of this book is tied up with match action with the emphasis solely on Goodison Park. The first ever League game is featured; the first League win; the first FA Cup success; the first European Cup game and so on. How did the fans react on those rare relegation days? What was it like at Goodison the day seven goals were scored before half-time? What was it like the day the immortal Dixie Dean made, not only his debut, but his final appearance? Historic matches, golden moments and also days of total despair. Forty-five very special games come under the microscope, spanning a century of Goodison glory.

Hopefully, your favourite encounter is amongst these pages. Even if it is not, there will almost certainly be reference to stars and personalities you particularly associate with.

This book could not have been written without the help of the 'Goodison watchers' who have gone before, not least my predecessors on the 'Liverpool Echo', 'Football Echo' and 'Liverpool Daily Post' whose reports and observations I have drawn on heavily during the compilation of this book. I speak particularly about the likes of Ernest Edwards ('Bee'), Bob Prole ('Ranger'), Leslie Edwards and in more recent years, people like Michael Charters.

A complete bibliography appears elsewhere, but first and foremost I would like to thank the 'Liverpool Echo' for allowing me access to their archives, as well as granting permission for the use of the vast majority of photographs that help to make this Goodison Park Centenary publication come alive.

Indeed, the first 'image' of Goodison comes in a rough sketch that appeared in the 'Football Echo' on 13 August 1892 — 11 days before the official opening. It is clearly not to scale in as much as the palings down the right (the Goodison Road side) are far too near the pitch, but it is nevertheless a fascinating insight into the thinking of the day. What was futuristic and spectacular to them, might seem plain and distinctly average to the fan of the late 20th century. But one should not overlook the fact that Goodison Park was the first major soccer ground to be developed in this country. Everton took the lead and the rest followed.

The 'Football Echo' carrying the sketch also described the ground in considerable detail. The 'prestige' covered stand, on what is now the Bullens Road side of the ground, accommodated the changing rooms and the various offices. The paper asked its readers to consider the achievement of the 'Young Everton party' in transforming the Mere Green Field into an exciting football venue in such a short space of time.

The report said: *The place has been transformed from a morass into one of the best appointed enclosures it is possible to clap eyes on; and all this has been done in the space which has elapsed since the last football season ended. That the committee of the Everton Club were put on their mettle in effecting such a change can be well understood by those who saw the wilderness at Goodison Road before the magic wand of Mr Kelly, the contractor, was passed over it.* (Ben Kelly would eventually become a club director).

The utmost credit is due to this gentleman for his work. He entered heart and soul into the undertaking and appeared inspired along with the committee of the club, in letting the cynics see what could be achieved.

The writer now compared the new venue to the former Anfield headquarters, declaring: *The ground is very extensive, perhaps too much so, and an ordinary crowd will almost get lost in it. It is capable of accommodating a couple of the old Anfield enclosures and then allowing room for knocking about. There is a stand* (now Bullens Road) *that goes nearly the full length of the field and is capable of seating, so Mr Kelly informs us, over 5,000 people. It is built gallery fashion so that every person who goes on it might have a comfortable and obstructless view of the game. They will also be well-sheltered from the biting east winds that are so prevelant during the football season. At the rear of this will be found a training track for the players which the 'sprinters' of the party will find very useful. Underneath the stand, all sorts of accommodating offices have been built. Here will be found well-appointed bathrooms, dressing-rooms, w.c.'s, storerooms, offices for the secretary and a private room for referees, access to the latter being made*

from the field of play. The players will not have to parade themselves through the public street, as was the case at Anfield Road, in all their 'War paint' and, what is of more importance, visiting teams will not have to 'run the gauntlet' through a crowd of incensed partisans whom they might probably have displeased in some manner on the field.

Here also will be found a telephonic apparatus, connecting the 'Football Echo' offices with the ground which will enable us to give the results of matches, as we did at Anfield, immediately the game finishes.

Prior to telephone contact, newspapers used carrier pigeons to get match information back to base.

The paper now described the goal ends, reporting: *At either end of the ground, strong, well-built galleries have been erected, computed to accommodate at least 10,000 persons and the Goodison Road side has been banked up in such a manner that from 15,000 to 18,000 people can arrange themselves along it in the face of the ornate stand opposite.*

In the centre of the Goodison Road cinder bank, set back against the walling of the ground, secretary Molyneux had another office. It was said that he sat here in his easy chair, writing cheques or keeping an eye on the extent of his vast domain. Chairman Mahon's seat on match days was directly opposite, on the far side of the pitch in the East Stand (Bullens Road). It was situated above the door and passageway that led to the changing rooms. There was standing accommodation in front of the East Stand.

The new pitch was said to be in top-class condition and ready to meet the hard work to which it would soon be subjected. The report said: *Most of the turf has been cut from Aintree. Many hundreds of cartloads of cinders have been brought in for draining and filling. On opening day, the place will be the finest, best-equipped and most comfortable football ground in the land.*

And so we have the perfect image of Goodison Park, 1892. If only those Goodison pioneers could stand in the centre-circle and cast their eyes around the place in 1992. I think they would be well satisfied that their labours led to something so very special.

George Mahon's Dream — And The 'Kicking' Of King John

GOODISON Park was England's first major football stadium. Officially opened on 24 August 1892, by that giant of the game Lord Kinnaird in the esteemed presence of Mr F. J. Wall, secretary of the Football Association, and Mr J. J. Bentley, president of the Football League, it inspired gasps of admiration from all those who saw it for the very first time.

One hundred years on, the proud home of Everton Football Club continues to set standards of excellence to retain its place as one of Great Britain's most spectacular sporting venues. The ground is very different today to the soccer citadel that rose out of a 'howling desert' which is how the original Mere Green Field was described prior to the royal blue pioneers turning it, almost overnight, into a football arena of character and quality.

Molineux, the home of Wolverhampton Wanderers, had been opened three years earlier, but was still fairly basic. Newcastle East End had become Newcastle United in 1892 and moved from their original Chillingham Road ground in Heaton to St James' Park, but it was little more than a field. Anfield, the ground Everton left behind on the other side of Stanley Park following a row over the rent, was but a shadow of its new rival. And so the Everton members and leading lights like George Mahon and Dr James Clement Baxter had every right to view their 'new baby' with a bursting pride, mixed with a sense of relief that the gamble to break free of the shackles of 'King' John Houlding, their former president and Anfield landlord, had been such a resounding success.

Early Everton historian Thomas Keates, who chronicled the club's first 50 years, and John Roberts, author of the official 'Centenary History' published in 1978, combine to give us a clear indication of the row that led to Everton turning their back on their Anfield home where they had played for nine years between 1884 and 1892.

Previously, of course, Stanley Park and Priory Road had played host to church team St Domingo and the Everton club it spawned in November 1879, at a meeting at the Queen's Head Hotel, Village Street, near the original Everton Toffee House.

Anfield had been a popular venue, but as Keates wrote: *A crisis in the club's affairs loomed in 1891, a smouldering fire that burst into flames.* He was referring to the increasing discontent amongst the members regarding the power game being played by Houlding, looked on either as the father of Association Football in the city, or a money-grabbing tyrant, depending on whose side you were on in an internal war that was accelerating to a climax early in 1892.

When the original move to Anfield took place, Houlding decided he was not only going to be the club's president, but also its representative tenant. The ground was but a short distance from the Sandon Hotel of which he was the proprietor. Club committee meetings were held there, the players changed there and Everton's various social gatherings were inevitably held within its walls. Many of the members, some of them still retaining strong connections with the St Domingo Church, objected to these powerful links with a drinking hostelry. But more than that, there was mounting resentment against Houlding.

The football field itself belonged to Mr Joseph Orrell and an adjacent field to Mr John Orrell, a brewer like Houlding. Joseph had given the club permission to use his field on the basis that 'the Everton Football Club keep the existing walls in good repair, pay the taxes, do not cause themselves to be a nuisance to Mr Orrell and other tenants adjoining, and also pay a small sum as rent, or subscribe a donation each year to the Stanley Hospital in the name of Mr Orrell'.

It was clear that he intended the club to benefit from any monetary advantage gained by the use of his field, an extremely generous gesture. But as soon as the prosperity of the new Anfield location seemed assured, Mr Houlding changed the ground rules and, instead of being the club's representative tenant, was suddenly their landlord. He intimated that as the Everton profits increased, so would the rent. It soared from £100 in 1885-86 to £240 in 1888-89 and then £250 the following year.

On 24 July 1888, the club's executive made a very sensible decision by refusing to spend funds on stands and expensive accommodation on the annual tenancy. Instead, they applied for a lease. Houlding immediately refused, but said that as long as the club paid a fair rent (or

George Mahon, whose vision and determination inspired the move from Anfield to Goodison Park.

his interpretation of a fair rent) and did not interfere with the boundary walls without his permission, he would not disturb the tenancy. At the same time, he added the rider that if any refreshments should be required on the Anfield ground, the landlord should have the sole right to supply them.

The complaints of the members flared into open anger. The men who would now prove inspirational leaders, the Mahons, Baxters and Claytons took centre stage.

They wanted to form the club into a Limited Liability Company for the express purpose of acquiring the Everton Football Ground (Anfield). This was put in the form of an official resolution at a special committee meeting held on 22 May 1889. It was going to be a long drawn out war of words — and deeds. Houlding and his supporters tried to take the upper hand with the trump card of possession. A general meeting was called on 15 September 1891 at the Royal Street Hall, close to Everton Valley, where Mr W.E.Barclay, a Houlding supporter, took the chair. He gave Houlding the floor and King John, after reading some letters from Mr Orrell's solicitor, now outlined his own plans for the formation of a Limited Liability Company. A prepared printed prospectus proposed the purchase of Mr Orrell's and Mr Houlding's land, and the stands, offices, etc., at a total cost of £9,237 10s.

Mr Barclay, after taking some questions, now proposed and Mr Howarth seconded a resolution: "That the scheme as explained be adopted." Now Mahon climbed to his feet. He put a bold amendment, seconded by Mr Montgomery: "That the scheme proposed be not entertained and that the committee have authority from this meeting to negotiate with Mr Houlding as to the renting of such further land as may be required, subject to Mr Houlding making the necessary arrangements with Mr Orrell." The amendment was carried.

There was now a succession of executive meetings and deputations without any progress being made. Mr Houlding sent a letter to the Committee

pointing out the existing conditions of tenancy. To try and head off the growing agitation for a move to a new venue, Houlding also made it clear that he would not give any undertaking whatsoever about the stands.

This new move was intended to be an effective obstacle to any change of ground, but it only served to fire up Mahon and his supporters. Keates has left us with a clear picture of Mahon's character and constitution. The man who, more than most, had a clear sight of a new beginning away from Anfield was respected as an accountant and a member of the Walton Local Board. By his own admission, he had been anti-football earlier in his life, but when he became the organist at St Domingo Church, he was gradually converted to the pastime being increasingly taken up by members of the congregation.

Bearded, extremely smart and articulate, Mahon inspired confidence in all those around him. His qualities as a fearless leader, some might call him a revolutionary, would now be put to the test. The 'split', as people now referred to it throughout the city, was looming large on the horizon. Keates summed up the intense pressure being put on key individuals like Mahon when he said: 'It involved considerable sacrifice of time, mental anxiety, diversion from their urgent business responsibilities, monetary risks, partisan denunciation and misrepresentation. The constructive responsibility entailed was intimidating; the finding of a new ground, the drudgery and expense of levelling, draining and sodding; the formidable items of stands, offices, dressing-rooms, etc., and of incalculable (in advance) tons of bricks, woodwork, roofing, were

Everton in 1889-90. Back row (left to right): D.Waugh (trainer), A.Hannah (captain), R.E.Smalley, D.Doyle, Mr R.Molyneux (secretary). Middle: A.Latta, J.Weir, J.Holt, G.Farmer, E.Chadwick. Front: C.Parry, F.Geary, A.Brady. While this happy group was being photographed at Anfield, trouble was brewing behind the scenes over the increase in rent.

13

enough to scare average men from the undertaking. But having voiced their discontent and dared the risky role of leaders, they shut their eyes to the consequences and the certain abuse that failure would ensure them'.

The time had now come, in Mahon's mind, to stop talking and take action. At a special general meeting at the College, Shaw Street, on 25 January 1892, it was once again made clear that a proposal to form the club into a Limited Liability Company, in accordance with Mr Houlding's prospectus, would not be entertained.

With the loss of the Anfield ground now a virtual certainty, Mahon played his ace card. He had been weighing up alternatives for some time and now spoke up about a possible new ground. A voice from the main body of the hall shouted: "Yer can't find one!" Mahon retorted: "I've got one in my pocket."

He was, of course, referring to Goodison Park, or the Mere Green Field as it was known at that moment in time. Those Everton stalwarts Dr James Clement Baxter and Mr W.R.Clayton now stood firmly by Mahon's side. They were an intriguing mix. If Mahon was the reasoned tactician, Clayton was the temperamental militant. As Keates wrote: *He added a dash of bitter to the mild.*

Dr Baxter was different again. He was said to have a sunny smile, a merry note and an optimism that improved his patients' well-being, not so much with a medicine bottle as with a cheery glance. He would prove to be Everton's 'Good Samaritan' in terms of easing their financial worries in those worrying times before and just after the opening of Goodison Park. But more of that later.

For now, the battle was still to be won with Houlding indicating that he fully intended to carry on with an 'Everton Football Club' at the Anfield ground. This now became the subject of a major dispute after it was learned that Houlding had registered a new company in Somerset House with the title of 'The Everton Football Club and Athletic Ground Company Limited'. The signature appended were Robert Berry, William (not John) Houlding, Alexander Nisbet, John James Ramsey, John Dermot, William Francis Evans and John McKenna. The battle lines were now firmly drawn up. Mahon knew exactly who and what he was up against.

There was much comment about the underhand way the new 'Everton' company had been registered without the full knowledge of the members and their committee. There were those who felt that Houlding had a case, but Mahon argued vehemently that his committee would fight tooth and nail to protect the interests of the majority of members who were clearly on his side. After all, there could only be ONE Everton, as laid down in the rules of both the Football Association and the Football League.

Messrs Clayton and Molyneux now attended a hearing in London at the Football Association's headquarters to settle the dispute once and for all. The FA Council adopted the following resolution: 'The Council, in accordance with its past decisions, will not accept

Everton in 1890-91. This was the year Houlding increased the Anfield rent to £250, infuriating the vast majority of club members. The team, meanwhile, got on with the business in hand. Back row (left to right): D.Waugh (trainer), R.Stockton (umpire), A.Hannah (captain), J.Angus, D.Doyle, R.Moly-neux (secretary). Middle: A.Latta, D.Kirkwood, J.Holt, W.Campbell, A.Milward. Front: A.Brady, F.Geary, E.Chadwick.

any membership of any club bearing a name similar to one already affiliated with this Association in the name of the Everton club, and will only recognise the action of a majority of its members at a duly constituted meeting.'

This resolution effectively wiped out Houlding's dream of carrying on with an 'Everton' of his own at Anfield. The Everton committee now met in February 1892, with Mr Jackson in the chair. Those present were Dr Baxter and Messrs Atkinson, Griffiths, Nisbet, Ramsey, Howarth, Stockton, Clayton, Carrier, Coates and Molyneux (secretary). Resignations were on the agenda and accepted from Houlding men, Barclay and Williams. Mr Nisbet then made an application, on behalf of Mr Houlding, that the book containing the list of members be sent to that gentleman. The request was supported by Mr Ramsey. Several members commented on the adverse attitude which Mr Houlding had assumed towards the club, and it was resolved to refuse the loan of the book.

Nisbet and Ramsey now came under intense pressure. Mr Clayton proposed that the action of the pair in supporting Houlding's claim to the name of 'Everton' should now result in a severe censure, and the resolution was carried. The majority of he committee went

further by declaring that they fully expected to have notice regarding the resignation of the president (Houlding) in time for the next meeting, as well as those of the people who had attached themselves to his interests.

Houlding would indeed be 'kicked out' with the whole city captivated by this very public battle. The meeting at which the Everton president would finally be declared 'Offside' took place on Tuesday, 15 March 1892. I particularly like the report carried in the subsequent edition of the 'Liverpool Review', a weekly publication described as being 'Of Politics, Society, Literature and the Arts'. The Everton business obviously came under the heading 'Politics'.

It said: *There is a terrible racket going on in Liverpool just now. The city, for all that is known to the contrary, may be on the eve of a dire calamity. It is not that Mr De Bels Adam is going to resign the mayoralty and be succeeded by 'Plain Joe' or that coal is going up to 30s an ounce, or that another line of pipes is to be laid down between Liverpool and Vyrnwy. These would be simple trifles compared to the catastrophe in view. H'sh! Break it gently, breath it with care, it is a football crisis, or, in other words, 'King Houlding' of Everton has been kicked. Not kicked physically, but kicked* out of the presidency and from the committee of the Everton Football Club. Circumstances have been leading up to this for a long time, and on Tuesday night the 'kicking' process came off amid a great deal of enthusiasm. Oh! football. There seems to be as much gratitude in you, in so far as 'King Houlding' is concerned, as there is for politics.

Years ago 'King Houlding' advanced the then struggling but rising Everton Football Club funds at a small rate of interest. He also assisted the organisation in other ways, for which the members were righteously thankful. As a landlord he lent the club a ground at a moderate rental to play on. He advanced money to erect grand stands, and provide all the rest of the paraphernalia of a first-class football club. Things went on swimmingly, and the Everton players made a name second to none in the football world. Then came a change of scene. Things were not what they seemed. As the club prospered, the rental of the ground increased, and the interest asked by the landlord for money advanced went up perceptibly. There were mumblings and grumblings, and finally the storm burst. 'King Houlding' insisted that he was in the right; the great majority of members insisted that he was in the wrong. The 'King' began to assert his power; his subjects broke out in open rebellion. Very soon it became a war to the knife.

On one side were the 'King', the sinews of war, and a small and chosen band; on the other side were a big army of malcontents. Fighting, armistices and strategems, first on the part of the 'King' and then on the part of the rebels, followed alternately. Finally, the 'King' has been 'kicked' and the victorious host have elected to migrate to pastures new and a fresh field, where a heavy rental will cease from troubling and the footballists will be at rest.

The 'Liverpool Review' now chastised both parties. It said: This business is very sad, and, as a large number of onlookers think, very stupid. There can be no doubt that 'King Houlding' has done a very great deal for the Everton Football Club, and no doubt the club has done something for 'King Houlding'. But neither of the contending parties seem prepared to admit this. 'The more foolish of them' say the onlookers. And it really is a pity that a man like

Lord Kinnaird, the most respected figure in the game, who officially opened Goodison Park on 24 August 1892.

Dr James Clement Baxter who eased Everton's financial burden during the move to Goodison in 1892. He served the club unrelentingly until his death in 1928.

'King Houlding' should be mixed up in such an unseemly wrangle as that which has been going on in Everton football for months past.

The 'Review' now posed an intriguing question as to the future and the possiblity of rivalries reaching fever pitch. It said: *The fat is in the fire now. There is just this to be said. Perhaps 'King Houlding' will run a new football club on the present Everton ground (Anfield). If he does, the migrators to the new ground in Goodison Road will have a rival bad to beat. The two organisations may prove more beneficial or more hurtful to local football generally than the one organisation under the old order of things. That remains to be seen. Meanwhile, the football loving public may anticipate the future outcome with perfect composure. One thing is certain, however. After the 'kicking' of Tuesday night it would appear to be hopeless to expect 'King Houlding' and the old Everton Football Club to come together again. To use a football term, 'King Houlding' is palpably offside. The organisation on Tuesday night numbered some 500 members, and of these only eighteen or 20 stood by the 'King'. The king is dead; long live the king'.*

This very colourful description of one of the most important meetings Everton have ever had highlights the remarkable level of support Mahon had from the grassroots membership. It was a case of: 'Power to the people'. There were a considerable number of Press reports suggesting that the whole affair somehow had political undertones. The lively 'Liverpool Review' belittled this idea in that same 1892 article, saying:

This unusual drawing depicts the sale of famous forward Jimmy Settle from Bury to Everton in 1898 for the princely sum of £400. Settle was the original goal-poacher, a skilful inside-forward who netted 97 goals for Everton between 1898 and 1908.

THIS FINE SETTLE WAS OBTAINED BY EVERTON FOR £400

The split is purely a business one. If not, why all the talk and twaddle about 'King Houlding' reaping incalculable wealth from his hotel (The Sandon), which adjoins the old ground; and why all the talk and twaddle about some other brewer or brewers finding the funds to open the new ground — brewers with tied houses in the immediate vicinity? Judging by the statements, pro and con, there would seem to be more beer than anything else mixed up with the row, though surely the game of football is not going to be prostituted as a means of selling XXX. This would be kicking 'offside' indeed'.

There is, of course, a certain irony about this last statement. Exactly 100 years on, in their Centenary season, the club formed at Anfield after Everton departed to Goodison Park, find themselves backed officially for the first time by a world-famous brewery! I suggest that Houlding, looking down from above, is well pleased. His old rival, Mahon, still conducting a heavenly battle of words, is almost certainly saying: "I told you so!"

Laughter, Hisses, Uproar — And A New Home!

WE CAN gain a fascinating insight into the meeting in which John Houlding — the Everton president, Anfield landlord and proprietor of the Sandon Hotel — was expelled from the presidency on 15 March 1892. The 'Liverpool Review', in its 26 March edition, carried some rough notes, written by one of the Everton members who attended that historic gathering. They capture the mood of the occasion perfectly.

8.05: Business starts. Houlding asked to take the chair. Won't. Minutes. Guarantee Fund. Hartley's amount received with loud shots of 'good old jam!' Hudson's with equally loud shouts of 'good old soap!' Chairman's speech. Lasts 40 minutes. In my opinion settles the matter at once. Members liability. Satisfactorily answered by Cornett. Tom Howarth rises and is received with cries of 'How many shares are they giving you?' — laughter, hisses, uproar, 'sit down', 'company', & few feeble cheers completely drowned.

9.00: All present wildly excited. Howarth fearfully and wonderfully interrupted as he wanders away from the question.

9.30: McKenna rises and is received with terrible howls of execration and yells of 'Lie down McKenna!' 'Traitor!' etc. This is kept up all the time he is on his feet. Is cried down. Cheers. Jumps up again. Howled down ditto. More

cheers. Howarth resumes, but is again interrupted. Members say he is only spouting to waste time.

9.45: Vote taken now for Goodison-road. No questions as to majority.

9.50: Mr Clayton moved that Mr Houlding, Howarth and Nisbet be removed. Nisbet says he will resign. Loud cries of 'We won't have it', 'We'll give you the sack' & Barclay says he would like to hear Mr Houlding defend himself.

10.10: Houlding's speech (the chairman hopes members will give him a silent hearing as he has been ill). This is given with but a few exceptions. General opinion of speech is that he might have treated communications as a gentleman should and have acknowledged the members.

10.25: Mr Houlding's speech lasted quarter of an hour. Wilson deeply regrets having to leave the old ground though the majority of the committee have his entire sympathy. Loud cheers and cries of, 'Good old Bob,' & Motion put to meeting. Honestly think there were not 50 voted against it (the move to Goodison). Howarth waits to speak, as regrets being removed from the committee. But meeting will not hear him. Motion as regards Ramsey. This seemed to ravel things.

Now 10.35: Members in hurry to close as there is only a few minutes to sup ale. Vote to chairman and loud cheering.

The Terms Of Settlement — And On To Goodison

ON 30 April 1892, it was reported in the 'Liverpool Echo' that there had finally been a settlement. The report said: *On Monday evening, a conference of representatives of the Everton Football Club and of the company recently formed with a similar title (*Houlding's Everton*) was held in the rooms of the Football Association, London, at which Mr Clayton presided. After some friendly discussion it was agreed to abide by the following terms of settlement:*

'The company to leave the name 'Everton' with the Everton Football Club, each side paying its own costs.

£250 to be paid to the Everton Football Club for all stands and hoardings as set out in the statement of claim — signed George Mahon (on behalf of the Everton Football Club), William Houlding (on behalf of the company). The new company has become affiliated to the Association under the title of Liverpool Football Club, and has now equal rights with any other affiliated body; and the long-standing dispute has thus terminated amicably.

Everton now prepared for the daunting task of turning the Mere Green Field into a major football ground in a matter of months. What is not widely known is that Mahon considered other possible venues, the main one being a plot of land a couple of hundred yards down Lower Breck Road, not too far from the present Liverpool Supporters' Club.

But Mahon had set his heart on the Mere Green Field, running alongside Goodison Road, and work would now start immediately to turn it into a first-class football ground. First of all, the debris was cleared away and a basic system of drainage carried out. At the same time, the surface was levelled and re-sodded. A Mr Barton agreed to do this on 29,471 square yards at fourpence-halfpenny per square yard. This was a formidable amount of initial expenditure. The club now employed Mr J. Prescott, a prominent local architect and surveyor. Historian Keates described him as a man who revelled in sport in his spare time and who lived in a fine old house on the border of the estate.

On 7 June 1892, a contract was made with Kelly Brothers, the Walton builders. They were instructed to erect two uncovered enclosures at the goal ends to accommodate 4,000 spectators each, and a covered stand to accommodate 3,000 fans, for £1,640 with a penalty clause in the event of non-completion by 31 July (the new League season was due to start on 3 September). On 20 June, another contract was made with Kelly Brothers to erect outside enclosing hoardings at a cost of £150. Twelve turnstiles were ordered at £7. 15s each and, on 9 August, a third contract was entered into for gates, sheds, etc., for the sum of £132 10s 0d, to be completed by 20 August.

Everton had £805 3s 0d cash in the bank, plus the £250 alloted by the FA for the properties left at Anfield. The limited company was formed with £2,500 in £1 shares and 2,212 applications for allotments represented £1,659. But Mahon still felt the worry of the financial outlay weighing heavy on his shoulders. As a leading city accountant, with offices in North John Street, he was a man of figures and everything needed to be exactly right. Fortunately, Everton were given a timely boost by one of their biggest supporters, Dr James Clement Baxter, who quietly advanced £1,000, free of interest and without asking for any security. And so the great challenge would be met and the new ground completed in time for the official opening on 24 August 1892, preceded by a celebratory dinner at the Adelphi Hotel.

George Mahon, the Everton chairman, presided over the VIP gathering and the principal toast, proposed by Lord Kinnaird, the game's most distinguished football figure, was: 'Success to the Everton Football Club.'

The formalities over, the guests now joined Mahon in a drive to Goodison Park in open-topped carriages. On reaching the Walton area, they were cheered by crowds of spectators, the local tradesmen literally putting out the flags to give the day a real carnival atmosphere. There were 12,000 spectators inside the ground and the very first Goodison roar now echoed around the new stands as his lordship declared the new stadium open.

Ironically, there was no football, but a varied sporting programme in which the club's own players participated. Lord Kinnaird started the first event by firing a pistol and the band of the 3rd Liverpool Regiment, conducted by bandmaster T.Rimmer, cheered the gathering with a lively musical programme. The day ended in spectacular fashion with fireworks exploding over Goodison Park.

The Mere Green Field would cost Everton £8,090. The total outlay in transforming it into a major football venue in the summer of 1892 was in the region of £3,500. The decision to actually purchase the ground was taken at a board meeting on 22 March 1895 with Mahon in the chair. It was proposed: 'That this meeting do approve of and adopt the contract entered into by the Everton Football Club Co Ltd on the 12th inst for the purchase of the Football Ground now used by the club. The resolution was carried unanimously.'

The Epitome of Contract indicated that the parties involved were Christopher John Leyland and Everton Football Club. Completion of purchase took place on 1 August 1895 and the mortgage was eventually cleared during 1904-05.

When Everton played at Anfield. The programme from a game against Glasgow Rangers in October 1886. The match was originally scheduled as an FA Cup game but became a friendly when Everton scratched because several of their best players were ineligible.

A Ground Fit
For Kings And Queens

THE NEW Goodison Park was so impressive that it was chosen as the venue for the 1894 FA Cup Final in which Notts County beat Bolton Wanderers 4-1. Improvements would now be made and, in 1895, a new Bullens Road stand was built at an outlay of £3,407. The original construction was perfectly adequate. Possibly the new work involved major spectator facilities. A further £403 was spent on roofing the Goodison Road side.

The club was amongst the richest in the land and a £3,718 profit was made following the successful 1906 FA Cup-winning campaign. They would now invest £13,000 in a double-decker stand at the Stanley Park End. Then, in 1909, a vast Main Stand emerged on the Goodison Road side of the ground. This new structure cost £28,000 and housed all the offices and dressing rooms. It survived until 1971 at which point it was completely demolished to make way for the present towering structure. Also

in 1909, £12,000 was spent on concreting the terracing and replacing the cinder running-track.

The 1909 main stand was one of the wonders of the sporting world. The architect was Archibald Leitch, whose trade mark was his criss-cross front balcony walls. An example of this can still be seen on the Bullens Road side of Goodison Park. The stadium was now so highly thought of that it hosted the 1910 FA Cup Final replay between Newcastle United and Barnsley, won by the Geordies. The attendance was 69,000.

Goodison Park got the seal of royal approval on 11 July 1913, when it became the first League venue to be visited by a ruling monarch. George V and Queen Mary were the honoured guests, inspecting local schoolchildren at the stadium. During World War One, the ground was used for army drill practice and there were other unusual visitors in the shape of US baseball

The tablet installed to commemorate the visit of the King and Queen in 1913. It can still be seen in the Main Stand, close to the 300/ 500 Club entrance.

25 March 1953, and the Everton and Fulham players observe one minute's silence at Goodison as a mark of respect for the late Queen Mary.

teams, the Chicago Whitesox and New York Giants. It is recalled that one player hammered a ball right over the Main Stand.

In 1926, a double-decker stand was built on the Bullens Road side of the ground for £30,000. Everton now picked up on an idea they had spotted during a trip to Aberdeen and installed dug outs at Goodison for the trainers, the first in this country.

Work was completed in 1938 on a new Gwladys Street stand, just in time for another royal visit, this time from George VI and Queen Elizabeth. This structure cost £50,000 and the stadium was now in magnificent shape, the first in the country to have four double-decker stands. The ground would subsequently suffer damage during

World War Two and the club received £5,000 for repair work.

The magnificent old main stand, so futuristic in its day, would now make way for the present Main Stand in 1971. The old structure had cost £28,000. The new one would top £1m. Eleven executive boxes would be sited along the front of the Main Stand in time for the 1981-82 season. There was standing in the Enclosure area in front of these boxes until the 1987-88 season when seats were installed to accommodate the ever-growing Family Club. The famous Gwladys Street terraces, the traditional home of the club's most vociferous supporters, became all-seater in time for the start of the 1991-92 season. Thus, Goodison Park became all-seater on three sides and the highly impressive venue we see today.

Minutes Leading To Golden Hours — And The Naming Of Goodison Park

GOODISON Park is a very different place today to the ground that rose on the Mere Green Field site in 1892. But there is still history all around you and the club retain the original minute books that reveal so much about those pioneering seasons prior to the turn of the century, not least the famous year of 1892 when George Mahon made the bold decision to give up Anfield and find a new home on the other side of Stanley Park.

To handle those books, still in perfect condition and all handwritten by Mahon and his colleagues, is a very eerie feeling. You can almost hear Mahon's confident voice speaking to you, powerful and full of hope for the future. He had led the 'split' from Anfield with allies like Dr J.C.Baxter, W.R.Clayton, A.T.Coates, J.Griffiths, J.T.Atkinson and J.Davies, men whose names would be found on the list of provisional directors on the prospectus of the Limited Liability Company into which the club was formed at Goodison Park.

It's worth dipping into those minutes books, particularly the volume for 1892, to pick out one or two gems of day to day business. For instance, there is a casual two-line reference in the minutes of the 27 June board meeting that is truly historic. Under the hand-written heading of *Name of Ground* it simply says: *Resolved the Football Ground be called Goodison Park.*

Prior to its development as a major football ground, the Mere Green Field had been a nursery which, it is said, had been sadly neglected and had turned into a 'howling desert'. It took its name from Mere Lane which ran between the old field and Stanley Park. There was another Mere Lane on the Anfield side of Stanley Park, off Robson Street and the City Engineers eventually eased the confusion by extending Walton Lane which originally ended at the top of Spellow Lane. Walton Lane now extended down as far as Queens Drive, as it does today, and so the old Mere Lane disappeared off the map.

Goodison Road and all the small terraced streets running off it were in existence when work was started on the new football ground in the summer of 1892. So it was a straightforward matter for Mahon & Co to call the stadium Goodison Park. There was no mystery or intrigue about it. The road itself was almost certainly named after a civil engineer by the name of George William Goodison who, in 1868 while representing the company of Reade-Goodison, gave a report on sewage to the Walton Local Board. By coincidence, Mahon would later become a member of the Walton Local Board, an enlarged parish council.

Mr Goodison was born in 1843 at Holbeck in Leeds, the son of Samuel, a milk seller, and Elizabeth. By 1881 he was resident in Hawkshead, Cumbria, and in 1886-87 in Monk Coniston, now Coniston, Cumbria. The Liverpool City Engineers street-naming department cannot confirm that Goodison Road was named after him, but research would seem to suggest that this is the case.

And so Goodison Park was officially, if not formally, named in the time it took Mahon to pen those two lines in the 1892 minute book. There were other matters of equal importance. For instance, it was resolved at the same June meeting that Mr Griffiths go to Scotland to sign on Dumbarton star Richard Boyle, a centre-half who would go on to make 243 rock-solid appearances for the Blues.

An indication of the wages paid at

that time came in a reference to Fred Geary, the club's ace marksman. It was resolved that he would be offered £3 per week during season 1893-94 with the net proceeds of a midweek benefit match adding to his salary.

Under the heading *Payments in Advance* it indicated that star outside-right Alex Latta was earning £3 a week while his teammate Edgar Chadwick was on only £2 10s (£2.50).

The following week, on 2 August, the minutes included a full list of forthcoming fixtures, other than Football League, with an indication of the gate receipts and guarantees on offer. For instance: *1 September, Bolton Wanderers (h) pay guarantee of £35; 19 September, Heart of Midlothian (a) Receive guarantee £50 plus half of everything taken over £100.*

Opponents in these various friendlies included contrasting names like Burton Swifts, Queen's Park, Newcastle East End, Grimsby Town, Middlesbrough Ironopolis, Liverpool Caledonians and Northwich Victoria.

On 4 August 1892, the directors met at Goodison Park, when it was resolved that the main club office be fixed near the gateway opposite Eaton Street on Goodison Road, elevated four feet and having an entrance from the road. One hundred years on, the main office is still opposite Eaton Street.

An unusual entry made on 8 August, 1892, concerned the appointment of a 'Rubber-down' who was presumably the club's first physiotherapist. The wages on offer were ten shillings (50p) a week and the man approached was a Mr S.Orme. Publicity was clearly top priority and it was resolved that certain members of the local Press would have their expenses paid to all away League matches and Cup ties. At this meeting, the club accepted Lord Kinnaird's offer to officially open the new ground on 24 August while deciding that the ceremony would include a sports day and firework display.

On 5 September 1892, just two days after the first-ever Football League game at Goodison Park (a 2-2 draw with Nottingham Forest), an entry appeared in the directors' minutes concerning *Soldiers, Police and Postmen.* It was resolved that these gentlemen, in uniform, be admitted free to the ground through the season-ticket entrance and that this fact be advertised. All one can assume is that the club felt that the presence of these 'uniformed' fans might be a good deterrent to any potential crowd trouble.

Admission prices were set at a meeting on 8 September 1892. For League and 'big' matches it would be 6d (2½p) for the ground, one shilling (5p) for the covered stand and the front of the same and two shillings (10p) for the reserved covered stand. Combination and small matches, half-price.

Everton were always quick to reward their players for outstanding work and, at the September 13th meeting, it was decided to pay each individual a bonus of ten shillings for the victory over Heart

A fine view of the old grandstand on the Bullens Road side which originally housed the dressing-rooms and various offices. This picture was taken around 1905.

of Midlothian. At the same time it was decided that 200 children from the local industrial schools would be admitted free to the next match, the Blues clearly looking ahead with a view to capturing the fans of the future.

An interesting 'minute' concerned the purchase of a horse for ground work. No automatic lawn mowers in those days! It was also decided that the team would be requested to purchase and wear blue stockings in the matches. How would modern players react to buying their own kit?

The links with the local Press continued to be nurtured. When the 'Liverpool Echo/Express' sought the use of the brand new Goodison Park for their annual Boxing Day match, the board readily agreed.

On 22 August 1894, with George Mahon in the chair, the minutes reveal that the rift with Liverpool Football Club had been healed to a degree. The split and the move to Goodison had caused a lot of ill-feeling. John Houlding — Everton's old landlord and 'master' — had formed his new club and gained admission to the newly-formed Second Division of the Football League. It was now resolved to send complimentary tickets to the directors of Liverpool FC, who were celebrating promotion to Division One.

The Anfield club's elevation to the top flight meant that the 'Cold War' would

One of Everton's stars when they first moved to Goodison was Fred Geary, the Dixie Dean of his day. He would return to Anfield in 1894 and end his playing days as a Liverpool player.

have to be brought to an end and Everton took the first steps with this hands-across-the-park gesture. All this is revealed thanks to the meticulous way the minute books were kept. The superb organisational qualities of the club's officers are there for all to see.

The Goodison Road side as it looked in 1905. Originally, this was just a cinder bank. A vast Main Stand was built along Goodison Road in 1909 which stood for the best part of 62 years.

Training For The High Standard Of Efficiency

WE ARE given a clear picture of the club's training methods during the early years at Goodison Park, thanks to a schedule that was drawn up by the secretary of the day, R.Molyneux. On 26 October 1896, on the orders of the directors, he issued each and every player with a printed card regarding the *Rules As to Training*.

Those rules are listed here as they appear on the card:

1. Monday — Walking exercises or Salt Water Baths.

Tuesday and Wednesday — Sprinting or Walking Exercises.

Thursday — Sprinting and Skipping Rope Exercises.

Friday — Walking Exercises.

A couple of swells – trainer Harry Cooke (right) and assistant trainer Bert Smith prepare for the 1929-30 season.

2. Every player must be on the ground not later than 10am and must sign his name in a book kept by the Trainer for that purpose (shades of that famous disciplinarian Harry Catterick 78 years later!) At this hour, such book will be removed and any Player whose name is not entered will be required to give the directors a sufficient reason thereafter.

3. Each player shall bring to the ground suitable clothing, necessary for the practice of the day.

4. The Players shall, if required by the Trainer, indulge in the practice of Football.

5. The Players shall undergo any other mode of training or practice as the Trainer may, under any circumstances, deem expedient.

6. The Players shall, so often as the Trainer may think desirable, take such medicines which are prescribed by the Trainer.

The Directors, in framing these rules, desire the co-operation of the Players in the observance thereof, and trust that the Players will assist them in maintaining the high reputation of the Everton Football Club by obedience to the commands of the Trainer in whom the

Tom Griffiths and Tommy White (left) enjoy a training session early in the 1929-30 season. Sadly, unhappy days were on the horizon, culminating in the club being relegated for the first time with a defeat against Sunderland in May 1930.

Local schoolchildren join in this summer training run along Queen's Drive in July 1953. Parker, Stewart (a new Canadian player), Farrell, Leyland, Lindsay, Easthope and Clinton are the Everton joggers. The footwear was very basic, a mixture of baseball boots, pumps and leather shoes. Clinton is wearing a pair of open sandels. No fancy training shoes in those days.

directors have vested the necessary authority.

The Directors look to the Trainer for the maintenance of the high standard of efficiency which the Players of the Everton Football Club have attained hitherto.

On occasions, the players were given special 'treats' at the discretion of the directors. Motor cars were few and far between in those days and so they were taken for a drive out into the greenbelt for tea, the greenbelt being places like Childwall, which are now so densely populated.

It's interesting to compare training *c.*1892 with the training of 1992. Howard Kendall painted me a picture of how the modern Blues prepare for a big match.

He said: "Training starts each day at 10.30am but many of the lads are out before then, doing their own stretching exercises or some weights. Many of them join together for a keep-ball routine in a circle or in pairs to help with their touch on the ball. It's all very light-hearted before we start in earnest.

"They get their legs going with a fairly long run and then it's into a stretching routine before the ball-work starts. The coaching staff make it as interesting as possible. Then the small-sided games begin and the goalkeepers are brought into it.

"If we are working on particular patterns of play, it's a case of going into a full game. There are quite a lot of finishing routines which are worked on. Training is obviously reduced as the week goes on and a match looms. When you are playing as often as we are now, you don't need to hammer people on the training ground. The games take care of themselves.

"Different clubs obviously have different routines, but ours involves a lot of ball-work. I know in the old days, the players rarely saw a ball in training. The idea was to make them hungry for it on a Saturday. But the game is a lot quicker now and that is reflected in the amount of work we do."

Howard Kendall describes how modern training is very different to the early days. He is pictured showing off the club motto: *Only the best will do.*

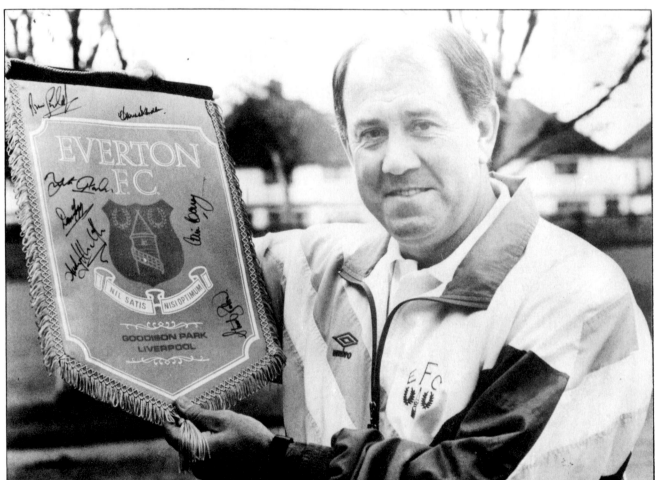

Hail Goodison, Hail Everton!

Saturday, 3 September 1892

Everton 2 Nottingham Forest 2

THE first game played on Goodison Park took place on Friday, 2 September 1892, when Everton entertained their old rivals Bolton Wanderers in a friendly encounter, winning 4-2. Fittingly, George Mahon was allowed to kick-off, a tribute to the visionary chairman. But this was only a warm-up act to the star turn, Everton's very first League match on their magnificent new ground against Nottingham Forest.

This fixture also marked the start of an exciting season and the fans who had been so used to wending their way to Anfield now swarmed to the new venue with great hope and expectation. The crowd was estimated to be in the region of 14,000, a magnificent turn-out considering the weather. The wind was blowing a gale and the rain was sweeping down, but the new pitch was in good condition.

The home team emerged first in their blue and white strip and they received a most enthusiastic welcome. Forest were also applauded warmly and promptly won the toss.

The 'Liverpool Football Echo' reported: *Little time was cut to waste and Fred Geary kicked off with a rush, but was well collared. Johnny Holt came in and enabled his partners to again move up, but Scott accounted for a dangerous move by the homesters.*

Holt was a powerful centre-half, virtually unbeatable in the air and nicknamed the 'Little Everton Devil' by his followers on the terraces. Thomas Keates explained why, saying that Holt was an artist in the perpetration of clever minor fouls.

When they were appealed for, his shocked look of injured innocence was side-splitting. In this opening League encounter, Holt was always to the fore.

Edgar Chadwick shot over the bar, but Forest stunned the home fans by taking

Richard Boyle played in Everton's first Goodison Park League game, a sturdy half-back who joined the club in 1890 from Dumbarton.

the lead. And so it was a Nottingham star with the unlikely name of Horace Pike, who had the honour of scoring the first League goal at Goodison Park.

Alex Latta now got stuck in and Alf Milward just failed to equalise after an outstanding cross came in from the right.

The previous year, Milward had been one of five Everton players to turn out for England against Scotland at Blackburn. He made a habit of confusing defenders with his rampaging runs down the left flank. Milward was a

Alf Milward made 27 League appearances in Everton's first Goodison campaign, scoring 11 goals. He was a skilful outside-left with an excellent football brain.

winner in every sense, never accepting defeat until the very final whistle, no matter what the score.

Geary now produced an outstanding leveller and Everton finished the half on the attack and in determined mood. On the restart, Chadwick and Milward both made some skilful runs and Latta distinguished himself with a stinging shot that dipped over the bar. Geary charged into Brown and a Forest player was cautioned after remonstrating with the referee.

Then Milward scored for Everton and

Higgins for Forest to leave the score level at 2-2, a disappointing result for the home fans who had been banking on Everton getting off to a flyer. But as they looked around their splendid new ground before wending their way home, they surely knew instinctively that great days and magical moments lay ahead. Goodison Park would prove a very happy home.

Everton: Jardine; Howarth, Dewar, Boyle, Holt, Robertson, Latta, Maxwell, Geary, E.Chadwick, Milward.
Attendance: 14,000

First League Victory At Goodison

24 September 1892

Everton 6 Newton Heath 0

EVERTON had kicked-off their very first season at Goodison Park with that 2-2 home draw against Nottingham Forest and had then lost 4-1 at Aston Villa and drawn 2-2 at Blackburn Rovers.

Now Newton Heath came to Merseyside for a clash that was causing great excitement amongst the Evertonians. They desperately wanted to see a Goodison triumph and felt the players were in the mood to see off the club that, ten years later, would take on the name of Manchester United.

The 'Liverpool Echo' reported the match in some depth. It said: *Newton Heath, one of the newest acquisitions to the League, were the visitors to Goodison Park and a large crowd assembled to witness the encounter. Amongst Evertonians, jubilation was great at the return to form of their pets, for they had gone to 'Auld Reekie' during the week and taken 3 to nil out*

of the formidable Heart of Midlothian, the leaders of the Scottish League. Their display in the Northern City was indeed powerful and finished and this being the first time the Hearts had been defeated on their own ground since April 1891, made the Everton victory all the more praiseworthy.

The question was asked: *Would the toffee boys maintain their form today and add a couple of points to their League credit?* The general opinion was in favour of a solid home victory as the Heathens had previously lost to Blackburn, drawn with Burnley and then succumbed to Burnley in an early return.

The weather was perfect when Fred Geary, the Dixie Dean of his day, kicked-off for Everton. Geary, a player who had scored a hat-trick on his England debut against Ireland in 1890, was renowned for his powerful running and finishing.

He was on the mark inside a minute and the fans in the new Goodison stand and enclosures erupted. The Newton Heath forwards now rushed down the field, but right winger Carson was dispossesed by Collins as he tried to thread his way through.

Geary, watching this spell of visiting pressure from the front line, now decided to do something about it and he claimed his second goal, taking a pass from the left wing and drilling in a low shot from long range. There was now a real spring in Geary's step and he made a magnificent run into the area, the move fizzling out through lack of support.

Edgar Chadwick now got on the scoresheet, a player who had signed for Everton from Blackburn Rovers in time for their inaugural season in the Football League in 1888. A mobile inside-left with a superb ability to read the game, he made a mockery of his slight frame (he was only 5ft 6ins) and was always in the thick of the action. His goal was well received and the home side were basking in a 3-0 lead.

But Newton Heath were still full of running and goalkeeper Pinnell had to punch clear from Mathieson. The second half belonged to Everton in every sense and they peppered the visitors' goal. Winger Alex Latta, who had the rare distinction of being a Scot and a tee-totaller, struck the crossbar with a fierce shot. Chadwick took the rebound and made it 4-0.

The 'Echo' now reported that the Evertonians *pursued their course merrily, constantly keeping their opponents on tenterhooks.* Maxwell and Milward completed the scoring as the home side leapt from 13th position to eighth. They would go on improving and finish a memorable first season at Goodison Park in third place, their home record being: Played 15, Won 9, Drawn 3, Lost 3.

There were also three Goodison victories in the FA Cup — against West Brom, Nottingham Forest and Sheffield Wednesday — prior to a three-match semi-final marathon against Preston North End that produced a Cup Final test against Wolves.

At Fallowfield, Manchester, Everton lost 1-0 to the Midlanders, but the fans could look back on a dramatic year. Their days at Anfield were now firmly behind them. Goodison Park felt very much like home and the club would go from strength to strength.

Everton: Pinnell, Howarth, Collins, Boyle, Holt, Robertson, Latta, Maxwell, Geary, E.Chadwick, Milward.
Attendance: 10,000

Southworth's Record Six-Goal Blitz

Saturday, 30 December 1893

Everton 7 West Brom 1

JACK Southworth spent a comparatively short time at Goodison Park, somewhere in the region of 15 months. But during this time, he managed to write his name into the Everton history books with his outstanding goalscoring feats. The six goals he plundered against West Bromwich Albion in 1893 still stands as the club's individual scoring record.

Southworth was described by respected judges as the best centre-forward of his era. He first played for Blackburn Olympic and at the tender age of 16, scored six goals for them against Leigh. He moved to Blackburn Rovers and when they crushed Sheffield Wednesday 5-2 in May 1890, it was Southworth who registered all the home goals.

His scoring feats came to the attention of Everton and they paid £400 for his services in August 1893, by which time the player already had two FA Cup winners' medals in his collection. The fee was a large one by the standards of the day, bearing in mind that it would be 12 years before the first ever £1,000 transfer was recorded (Alf Common from Sunderland to Middlesbrough in February 1905).

Southworth scored on his debut at the County Ground, Derby, although the Blues lost 7-3. But he would soon be making his presence felt in a big way and hit four in an 8-1 demolition job on Sheffield Wednesday.

The following week he would go two better and score his record-breaking double hat-trick against West Brom. The Throstles didn't know what hit them on a foggy Goodison Park afternoon.

Creative right winger John Bell, a player with a fascinating background in his own right, scored in the opening minute. The Scot had won a League Championship medal with Dumbarton before joining the Blues in 1892. He was chairman of the first attempt to form a players' union and is reputed to have once saved the life of a fellow First Division player by repositioning a dislocated neck with a wrench of his powerful hands. Bell, having scored against West Brom, now turned creator with an accurate centre that Southworth headed home.

Jack Southworth scored six goals against West Brom in December 1893, to set an individual club record.

The same combination produced the third goal, Reader failing to hold Bell's shot and Southworth racing in to make it 3-0. The unstoppable centre-forward then scored an outstanding individual effort to complete his hat-trick, dribbling the ball into the centre and powering home a shot.

The crowd was increasing by the minute, along with the score. In those

John Bell's skilful dribbling down the right flank thrilled the Goodison fans and helped Jack Southworth claim his record-breaking six-goal haul in 1893.

of course, are figures estimated by the reporters of the day, but they had a keen eye and were usually spot on with their guesses.

Bell continued to thrill the crowd as much as his famous teammate. He dashed clear and Southworth joined him in the area to finish off the move and make it 5-0. Norman pulled one back for the visitors, but Southworth's strong shot made it 6-1. He was now on the brink of a double hat-trick and achieved it after meeting a Latta free-kick from the right.

In modern times there would have been pictures galore, quotes and headlines as big as your fist to salute such an achievement, but the coverage was much more modest in those early days.

The 'Football Echo' headline, across a single column, simply said: *Everton v West Bromwich Albion, League Division One.*

But it did not need fancy words to explain the way the fans thought of Jack. Sadly, injury and illness brought his career to a premature end. He finished the 1893-94 season with 27 goals in 23 games and managed nine in nine matches the following year before he was forced to retire.

He would remain a great entertainer, although he would earn his applause on a very different stage. Southworth was an accomplished violinist and he became a professional musician, being good enough to join the famous Halle Orchestra. But it was the roar at Blackburn and Goodison that had been music to his ears. He will be remembered, first and foremost, as one of the deadliest strikers in the business.

Everton: Williams; Parry, Arridge, Kelso, Holt, Stewart, Latta, Bell, Southworth, Chadwick and Milward.
Attendance: 14,000

days, because of people's working patterns it was often impossible to make the kick-off. Hence, there were 12,000 in Goodison at the start of the match, 18,000 present by half-time and up to 25,000 in the ground by the end. These,

THE BIG BATTLE AT LAST !

EVERTON *versus* LIVERPOOL.

THERE are some people in this world who are foolish enough to hold in light esteem, to speak words of scorning of, and to elevate their noses at, a pastime which has been known to

lists against his formidable enemy, all the city is agog to know whether he will be able ⸱⸱ ⸱⸱ down his man.

For after the split of 1892, h⸱ ⸱ new have " got on "

popularise " the great game " amongst classes of our community. Mr. Mahor of a firm of N⸱ ⸱ ⸱ ⸱ n-street solicito

Houlding Kicked Again — In The First 'Derby'

The nearest you will get to a sensational headline in 1894. How the 'Liverpool Review' previewed the first-ever Football League derby, played at Goodison in 1894.

13 October 1894

Everton 3 Liverpool 0

EVERTON'S 1892 departure to Goodison Park led to the formation of another team in the city. Anfield landlord John Houlding, having been 'kicked' out of the Everton presidency during the historic 'split', now found himself guiding the fortunes of the new Liverpool Football Club.

They had siezed the opportunity to play in Second Division of the Football League in 1893-94 and gained promotion at a gallop after winning 22 of their 28 games and drawing six.

And so in early October 1894, the only topic of conversation on Merseyside was the impending top-flight battle at Goodison Park between George Mahon's Everton and Houlding's Liverpool — the very first League derby. Newspapers were not in the habit of sensationalising things in those days, but here was the ultimate sporting battle. The game was given a full-page spread in the 13 October edition of the 'Liverpool Review' and they made no apology for 'going over the top'.

The article said: *There are some people in this world who are foolish enough to hold in light esteem, to speak words of scorning of, and to elevate their noses at, a pastime which has been known to draw together at one assemblage a vast congregation of persons numbering between forty and fifty thousand strong, amply sufficient to people a good-sized town or a fairly formidable army. None of these superior creatures will be discovered at Goodison Park on Saturday afternoon and none of these people will be missed. A man who can wax sarcastically superior to the hundred and odd thousand sport-lovers who crowd the football enclosures of the United Kingdom every Saturday is altogether too elevated for common comprehension.*

He is a chap no fellah can understand. So we will not apologise to Mr Minority for having introduced so much football fare into this issue of the 'Review'. Our end is to entertain the thirty thousand odd footballists who will throng the great Goodison enclosure on Saturday afternoon. For the hour of the big battle has arrived, and Everton and Liverpool are to meet — at last!

The second teams of the two great rivals had met in the Liverpool Cup, each claiming a victory. But there had been no clash of first teams, basically because Everton believed they were of far superior stock to the new occupants of Anfield.

The 'Review' explained: *Whenever local competitions made it necessary for the clubs to meet, the Evertonians would not condescend to place more than their second string in the field against any kind of string of Liverpudlians, against which treatment the Liverpudlians*

35

Billy Stewart was a solid half-back who joined Everton in 1893 from Preston North End. Billy was a long-throw expert, although his running and jumping routine was later outlawed.

naturally stood on their dignity by sending only their second string, with the consequence that the clubs never representatively met — until now!

Because here was a First Division fixture that required and received the total attention of both parties. The 'Review' was reluctant to predict a result, although Everton were most definitely the form favourites. They topped the table, having played seven and won seven. Liverpool had played eight, won none, drawn five and lost three. But they were fired up as they had never been before. These days we talk about the 'old enemy'. In 1892 it was simply the 'enemy'.

The 'Review' provided pen pictures of the leading characters. George Mahon, now the president of Everton, was said to be a man whose tact and business ability made him an invaluable member of the Everton organisation. His presence was welcomed in all football circles and his association with the leading men of the city made him a perfect emissary for the game amongst the influential members of society.

Jack Southworth was the captain of the League leaders, described as the most famous centre-forward living. James Adams was Everton's sub-captain. Signed from Hearts, he was a solid full-back with a perfect physique.

The opposing ranks had a familiar overlord in John Houlding. Once Everton's chief mainstay, his decision to increase the Anfield rent had led to the parting of the ways. He had survived the 'split' to build a new Anfield team and he was desperately keen for Liverpool to beat the Blues, especially at Goodison Park.

Andrew Boyd Hannah was the skipper of the Anfield club. He was perhaps the most familiar soccer figure in the city, having captained Everton previously. He was a model full-back, steady, reliable and cool. He was backed up by Jimmy McBride, one of the smallest, but pluckiest half-backs in the League.

And so to the game itself. For hours on the Saturday afternoon, Scotland Road was congested with vehicles of all sizes. There was an endless supply of cabs and hansom carriages, backed up by scores of buses and trams which were besieged by the multitudes heading for Goodison Park. The approaches to the ground, said the 'Liverpool Review', seethed with struggling humanity for hours before the event.

The magnificent football arena presented a spectacle imposing in the extreme. It only needed a glance at the packed masses of spectators rising tier above tier in every quarter of the enclosure to make even the most hardened footballer utter expressions of astonishment at the drawing power of the great game.

The form book proved to be right. Everton won 3-0, although the visitors managed to carve out a considerable number of chances. Up to the last half hour, it was anybody's game. The 'Review' observed: *If Liverpool were a*

little less unscrupulous in their tactics, they would be a popular team.

Houlding's men were very physical and two-thirds of the fouls went against them. Liverpool's kick and rush tactics had disrupted a number of teams, but Everton had too much quality.

Blues' winger John Bell limped off after some over-zealous tackling from his marker, but he soon returned to a deafening roar of approval. The lead was secured when Hannah handled and McInnes headed home Stewart's excellent free-kick.

But it was just 1-0 at half-time and Liverpool made a robust start to the second period without having any luck in front of goal. Then Alex Latta whipped in a powerful shot and it was 2-0. Bell finished off the battling visitors

when he chested home a right-wing cross and the Blues had made a record start to a campaign with eight wins from eight games, scoring 30 and conceding only seven.

Sadly the run came to an end in the following game at Blackburn and the side finished the season as First Division runners-up to Sunderland.

But the most important thing as far as the fans were concerned was that Liverpool had been well beaten at Goodison. Less than a month later, the Blues returned to their old Anfield home and secured a 2-2 draw. Houlding would have to wait some considerable time for his revenge.

Everton: Cain; Adams, Parry, Boyle, Holt, Stewart, Latta, McInnes, Southworth, Hartley, Bell.

Attendance: 44,000

Shouts, Shrieks, Groans, Cheers — And Then Handshakes All Round!

EVERTON'S second season at Goodison Park, 1893-94, was very much a mixed bag. The Blues, having finished third the previous year, now went backwards and dropped to sixth. They also crashed out of the FA Cup at the first time of asking to Stoke. But there had been much to admire as well. This was the year in which Jack Southworth bagged his six goals against West Brom, a feat that still stands to this day as a club record. The Blues won that match by 7-1 and twice recorded 8-1 triumphs, against Darwen and Sheffield Wednesday.

And yet there was a little bit of in-fighting going on behind the scenes, a mini power battle that would reach a climax at the club's annual general meeting, held in the imposing Picton Lecture Hall. It was a gathering that started in explosive fashion and then really warmed up! Shareholders meetings are traditionally occasions that can turn mere mortals into raging bulls. Football, like religion and politics, can prove to be a dangerous subject on which to air extremist views.

Football is a passionate game, even on a bad day. At this particular share-holders' meeting, with vacancies on the board the main topic of conversation, it was not so much pistols at high noon, as a display of sabre-rattling throughout the night.

I reproduce below every dot and comma from a report of the proceedings, written by a gentleman calling himself 'The Linesman' in the 'Liverpool Review'. It is a most wonderful piece of descriptive writing, significant because it reveals the debating skills of one George Mahon — the man who led Everton from Anfield to Goodison. There is also reference to a 'Mr Keates', who distinguished himself at the meet-ing with his sound oratory in the face of tough opposition. Could this have been the famous Goodison historian Thomas Keates, whose most superb 'History of Everton Football Club' was published in 1929, leaving us with so many valuable memories about the early Blues? It is an intriguing thought.

But back to the June meeting of 1894. Present shareholders will, I am sure, enjoy the report, taken from the old 'Liverpool Review'. It's a classic example to any would-be journalist of how to paint a picture with words. We thank 'The Linesman' and salute his writing prowess. This was his report:

On Monday evening, at the Picton Lecture Hall, the long expected thunderbolt was hurled, and nobody was killed. But there were great ructions all the same, and many a time during the three hours' sitting of the directors and shareholders of the 'igh and mighty Everton Football Club a 'fite' appeared imminent. But it is all over now, and, as I say, nobody is assassinated. On the contrary, the whole club is decidedly the better for an annual meeting which commenced rumblingly, continued with shouts, shrieks, groans, hisses, pale faces, and personalities, and concluded with humorous speeches, facetious commentaries, votes of thanks, congra-tulations, and hand-shaking all round. After which let us hope that patriotism will take the place of dissension amongst the members so the Everton FC, and that the coming season will see better management, better results, and hatchets buried by the score.

To a disinterested onlooker the proceedings in the Picton were of a most humorous description. A spectator who knew not football would probably have been amazed at the intensity of interest displayed by the five or six hundred club members who for three hours howled and gesticulated themselves blue in the face, Everton-blue in the face, over the affairs financial and governmental of their body. Personally, it was the most entertaining partisan experience which I have come across since Liverpool beat Everton at Hawthorne Road in the final for the Liverpool Cup in 1893.

It really was great fun. On the platform there sat Mr George Mahon, chairman of the meeting and president of the club. On his left was Mr Molyneux, and on his right Mr Clayton, and in the rear a number of directors. The shareholders were mostly seated in the body of the hall, but grouped on a tier of seats to the right, and facing the platform was a partisan body whose business it appeared to be to play the very holocaust with the directorate in the way of criticising its management, to push forward certain members of its party for the vacancies which had occurred amongst the directorate, and to vigorously protest against the right to vote of certain newly acquired shareholders and members of 'the trade'.

Thus we had the elements of a nice little thunderstorm, and little time was wasted in getting to words. The chairman, a thin little man with a caustic tongue and a personality powerful enough to keep the riotous spirits at his fingers' ends from first to last, confessed right away that he was in a bad temper, and then proceeded to make the best that was possible of the clubs' finances for the past season, which he admitted he expected would be warmly discussed. These he got through with fairly little interruption, but when he came to the subject of certain by-meetings which had been held by the afore-described factionists, the storm which had long been brewing burst forth in all its frenzy, and almost shook the volumes in the huge library above out of their shelves.

It was very warm indeed. Mr Mahon said that the test of the problem lay to his mind in the question: Were or were not such meetings to the advantage of the club? Whereat he was greeted with a perfect bombardment of 'Hear, hears, noe's' and 'Ayes'. And the state of things

was not improved when he proceeded to name the leaders of the factionists, and expressed it as his opinion that 'Messrs. Nelson, Green and Wilson would woefully regret that they had allowed their names to be brought forward at the meeting to receive such scant support:' and he trusted they would in future have a little more modesty, which would certainly be an advantage both to themselves and the Everton club. In fact it was a vigorous speech altogether, and at times the speaker carried the audience with him to such an extent that they cheered him again and again, expressing their approval in such cries as 'Bravo, Mahon!' 'Good old chairman!' and so on. All of which approvalisms were levelled truculently at the factionists, who sat with their faces set loweringly towards the directorate on the platform and the stormy mass in the body of the hall.

And then one of the leaders of the minority party rose to his feet, and was

Thomas Keates, author of the invaluable 'History of Everton Football Club 1878-9 to 1928-29', who died in his 79th year while the volume was in process of publication. Keates was a former director. Was he also the man who challenged George Mahon from the floor at the 1894 annual meeting? It is a fascinating thought.

rewarded with a roar of mingled hoots and cheers such as that which used to greet the name of Gladstone at the pantomime, only more so. Mr Keates was the would-be speaker; a middle-aged man with a bull-doggy countenance and a voice which would have done justice to a ship's captain. 'In a friendly way' (which was obviously a very iconoclastic way) he desired to discuss the statement of accounts which had just been approved and passed. He talked, between the whirlwinds of hooting and jeering, of the high expenditure re players; of the injurious nature of the bonus system; and of the threatened rivalry which they had to fear from a neighbouring club. He contended in opposition to the chairman that the directorate lost nothing by being subjected to such criticism as that which he and others had brought forward; and altogether Mr Keates fought so well in the teeth of the wind that several times the meeting heartily echoed his sentiments, and the three gentlemen at the table on the platform visibly appreciated the Cromwellian attack. Mr Keates subsequently distinguished himself by rushing on to the platform with a letter from a firm of lawyers, handing it triumphantly to a director in answer to a point of legal difference which had arisen, striding up to the chairman's table, seizing a glass of water and gulping the contents down, and then striding back to his place in the arena as quickly as he came. This feat simply brought down the house, and probably will have immortalised Mr Keates in the Extraordinary Annals of the Remarkable Football Club of Everton.

Mr Keates was seconded by Mr Fisher, at whose up-rising the sensation was even more tremendous, for it was evidently anticipated that this gentleman meant business, Mr Fisher had not quite the bull-doggy appearance of Mr Keates and his diction was a trifle more refined, but if anything he was even more energetic. He was a born orator, suiting the word to the action, the action to the word with a facility and effectiveness which electrified his hearers. Mr Fisher had very great difficulty in

making himself heard. He evidently had something to say which the majority of the audience didn't like to assimilate, but in spite of the opposition he stood his ground, and waving his arms and shaking his first utterly defied his antagonists to shift him from his position. It was no use trying to howl him down, for howling wasn't controverting, and they were facts, facts, facts, beastly, Gradgrindish facts, which he had to retail. In his opinion a crisis had been caused in the affairs of the club by the manipulation of paper shares and the distribution of scrip among 'the trade'. There! It was out! The trade! what trade? 'Tell us the trade,' they roared; and a rotund gentleman at the speaker's side grew absolutely purple at the insinuation, and threatened the plucky speaker with all sorts of dire mishaps. But, bless them, the imperturbable Fisher was not to be daunted, and he told them 'what trade'. He referred them to the meeting which took place at the Star and Garter at half-past seven; at which kind reference the disorder grew so awful that even Mr Fisher had to sit down.

Here the Chairman interposed, looked round at the clock, and thought it would be as well if they did a little business by way of relaxation — the election of three new directors, six being nominated on the spot. But before this was proceeded with, Mr Clayton, a dark-faced, long-faced, eloquent young man, rose from his seat at the side of the chairman, and in a big voice which made the ashphalt flooring quiver, proceeded to butter a couple of the directors, of whose merits he appeared to think the meeting was not becomingly cognisant. His speech was greeted with sympathetic applause, and at the conclusion the chairman added to the two directors mentioned the name of Dr Baxter, regretting that Mr Clayton had omitted a pat of butter for that popular gentleman, the reference to whom was received with unbounded delight. To this Mr Clayton rose to respond, whereupon a little gentleman from the rear of the writer, who had been indulging in sententious but somewhat silly asides

The colourful 1894 annual meeting featured the superb debating skills of Goodison founder-father George Mahon, who was backed by the likes of W.R.Clayton and Dr.J.C.Baxter. Three influential Evertonians were still in high office when this photograph was taken in 1906 with the old FA Cup. Back row (left to right): A.R.Wade, W.C.Cuff, Dr Baxter, D.Kirkwood. Front: W.R.Clayton, B.Kelly, E.A.Bainbridge, George Mahon, Dr W.Whitford, R.Wilson.

throughout the evening, called upon the speaker to 'sit down', which so roused that gentleman that he turned his long dark face full upon his interrupter and exclaimed that he wasn't going to sit down for a new *shareholder, not he; that he had worked morning, noon and night for the club before the said shareholder was dreamt of; which retort was received with a hurricane of applause, although the sat-upon gentleman looked daggers at the dark-faced director, and eventually, I have reason to believe, called him out for a duel, to take place in the Goodison ground Press Box, with Mr Mahon as referee and Mr Wilson (who reminds me of Cattermole every time I look at him) as goal-keeper.*

But this is getting a bit mixed, as Mr Mahon said at 10.30, when two hours and a half had gone and no work had been done, and he felt tired. So the voting was proceeded with (by ballot), and while the scrutineers were scrutineering the flimsies, which took them an hour to do their satisfaction, the audience congratulated itself all round upon the happy termination of the blow-up, and hoped things would go on all the smoother for it, as indeed I hope and expect they will. The man with the lion voice extracted a vote of thanks for the directorate, which request

was responded to with all the jollity imaginable, for all the world as if the said directorate had been the best boys possible, and had done everything they would have done and nothing they should not.

Then it was announced that the voting was as follows: Mr Wilson, 254; Dr Baxter, 239; Mr Leyland, 204; Mr Brooks, 170; Mr Davies, 105; and Mr Bainbridge, 100; Messrs Wilson, Baxter, and Leyland being accordingly elected.

Mr Secretary Molyneux added an interesting item to the proceedings by giving the names of the players for the coming season, these being received in silence, without sign of approval or the other thing. The names are:

Goalkeeper: Cain, R.Williams, and Jardine (as an amateur); full-backs: Adams, Kelso, Parry and Arridge; half-backs: Boyle, Holt, Stewart, Walker and Storrier; forwards: Latta, M'Innes, Southworth, Hartley, Chadwick, Milward, Bell, Geary, Reay, Murray, W.Williams, M'Millan, and Elliott.

And that's all. I have tried to reproduce for your benefit a spice of the enjoyment which I experienced at this Annual meeting of the Everton Football Club. It was very amusing indeed, and a little thrilling at times. Seriously, though, I believe the blow-off has done the club all the good in the world.

The Goodison Turnstile Fraud of 1895

In the early days, local reporters estimated attendances with quite remarkable accuracy. This pre-World War One group includes John Wolfe of the 'Liverpool Daily Post' (fourth from left) whose son Harold later gave sterling service to the 'Liverpool Echo' sports desk. John Wolfe could recall the days when pigeons were used to rely information back to newspaper offices. It was the gate-guessing expertise of such Press men that led to the unearthing of the 1895 Goodison Park Turnstile Fraud.

FOR some time prior to the 1895-96 season, the club's Finance Committee were concerned about the amount of gate money being handed over in relation to the number of people in the ground. Estimating crowds was a national pastime in those days and directors and reporters alike were expert at it. They could usually tell you before the end of any game what the official attendance would be, simply by casting an experienced eye around the various enclosures. They were never very far wrong.

But around this time, estimated attendances suddenly began to differ wildly from the figures being shown on the turnstile 'counters'. The money always tallied with the turnstile numbers, but there was this 'gut feeling' that many more people were in the ground than the 'official' figure suggested.

The turnstiles were fairly new and of a good make. They were checked regularly for any minor flaws. And yet there still seemed to be this anomaly. It was possible that an operator might be sixpence or a shilling short at times by giving the wrong change, but it appeared to go much deeper than that.

The club hated the idea of any of their

men being dishonest. It was felt that there might be a major fault with the turnstiles and so it was decided to check things out at the next big match, against Sunderland on 12 December 1895. Mr John Davies, one of the oldest and most respected of the directors, went around as usual with the groundsman half an hour before the gates were opened and took the numbers.

But 20 minutes later, ten minutes before the gates opened, Dr Baxter made a second check with Mr Davies. With their own key, they checked the numbers already noted, which should have been the same.

The results were startling. In quite a number of the stiles, the 'clock' had been put back 200 units. Yet no one appeared to have access to them and only the groundsman had a key. One employee was questioned and taken to Westminster Road Bridewell and detained. Meanwhile, the men went as usual to their allotted stiles and the gates were opened to the public. Watching

every money taker was a plain-clothed officer and when the gates were finally closed, seven men paid in exactly £5 more than their stile registered.

The trick was clear. Having been put back 200 units, it would take 200 sixpences — amounting to £5 — before registering against the stile operators. But each man questioned still pleaded ignorance and it was not possible at that stage to charge anybody.

The fraud was finally solved when the young employee at the Bridewell confessed, implicating over a dozen stilemen and the mechanic whose job it was to repair the stiles. The groundsman, the man whose duty it was to check the stile numbers with a director before and after each match, was also involved. That evening, and in the early hours of the following morning, 15 individuals were arrested.

The famous Everton Turnstile Fraud had been solved and it led to a brand new type of machine being introduced soon after.

The Goodison Park Riot

28 December 1895

Everton 0 Small Heath 0
(abandoned after 30 minutes)

DECEMBER of 1895 will go down as one of the maddest months in the history of the Everton club. For no sooner had the 'Turnstiles Fraud' been solved, than a riot unfolded on the day of the First Division game against Small Heath, the club which later became Birmingham City.

The date was 28 December 1895, and the big game coincided with one of the wettest spells for some considerable time. It had rained non-stop for three days and the Goodison pitch was heavily waterlogged in the morning.

There was much confusion as to whether it would drain in time, but when the gates were eventually opened at the normal time in a torrent of rain, the referee seemed quite satisfied that the pitch was playable. But a large number of supporters, fearing a postponement, stayed away and the attendance at kick-off time was around 6,000, only one-third of the average.

Play was farcical from the off. The players were slipping and sliding and the heavy ball was immovable at times. The players stuck at it for 30 minutes before the official signalled a halt and pointed to the dressing-room.

The crowd remained fairly patient for 15 minutes, waiting for a restart. The people in the seated areas, accepting nothing could be done, began to disperse. But a small section of fans made their way to the club office and demanded their money back. What was not clear was exactly how many of these people had paid to get in. Did they include late-comers?

The secretary tried to make himself heard from the balcony, but someone aimed a stone at him. Then the senior director, George Mahon, tried to get a hearing. He offered to give everyone present a free ticket for when the game was replayed, but the mob wanted money, not tickets. A stone shattered the glass of the large clock above Mr Mahon's head. A shower of missiles followed and the police immediately sought help from Dale Street headquarters. Sections of the palisading were ripped away and the staves used as weapons.

Every pane of glass in the pavilion was shattered. Meanwhile the 'rioters' began to march over the pitch and clamber into the stands, causing damage all the way. Others made for the dressing-rooms and there was even a shout to 'fire the stands'. Many of the police had head wounds, but they held their line to prevent the mob from reaching the main offices.

The police reinforcements suddenly arrived and, on command, drew batons. The crowd still seemed in the mood for a fight, but soon they were on the run, swept from the main gate near Spellow Lane. Goodison Road was cleared and the Everton riot was over. A small force of police were left on duty at the ground to retain the peace of the area overnight.

The game was eventually replayed on 3 February 1896 — on a Monday afternoon — and some 8,000 spectators saw the Blues win 3-0 with goals from Hartley (two) and Goldie to lift Everton to second place in the table. They eventually finished third.

Everton's Biggest Ever First Division Victory

Monday, 3 September 1906

Everton 9 Manchester City 1

DOWN the years Everton have had their fair share of runaway victories. In 1889 they beat Stoke 8-0 in a highly one-sided Football League encounter. They crushed Plymouth Argyle 9-1 in the Second Division in 1930 and put eight past Southampton without reply in a memorable Division One clash in 1971.

On the FA Cup front, an 11-2 success over Derby County raised more than a few eyebrows in 1890 and an 8-0 League Cup win over Wimbledon in 1978 and 5-0 UEFA Cup rout of Finn Harps the same year are also worthy of mention.

But it is the 9-1 hammering of Manchester City on 3 September 1906 that is rated as the club's greatest scoring achievement because of the game's top-flight status. And the players who produced the goods so magnificently at Goodison Park were members of one of Everton's greatest-ever teams.

In goal was Irishman Billy Scott, whose younger brother Elisha would become a legend in his own right across the park at Anfield. Billy was Everton's custodian in the 1906 and 1907 FA Cup Finals and he won three League Championship runners-up medals. Two local men filled the full-back berths, Walter Balmer and Jack Crelley. Balmer, whose younger brother Robert also played for the Blues, was famous for his powerful tackling and he represented England and the Football League. Crelley, although a Merseysider, arrived at Goodison from Millwall.

The vastly experienced half-back line consisted of Walter Abbott, Jack Taylor and Harry Makepeace, a truly outstanding trio in any company. Abbott had joined the Blues in 1899 and he flourished as a hard-shooting left-half. He was one of the original marathon men, covering every inch of the pitch. Taylor was one of the old school, a versatile character who arrived at Goodison in 1896 and played in the 1897

Left: Jimmy Settle, a classy inside-forward with an eye for a goal, who was on the mark when Everton beat Manchester City 9-1 in 1906.

Right: Centre-half Jack Taylor was not just a steadying influence in Everton's biggest-ever First Division victory in 1906. He also scored the first of the Blues' nine goals.

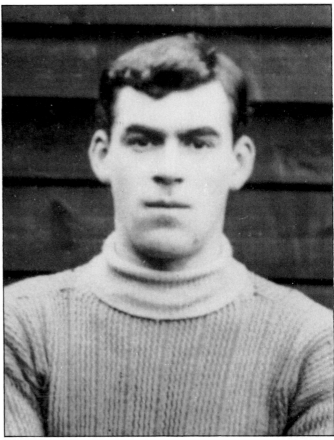

Cup Final on the right wing. He was still going strong when Everton reached the Final in 1906 and again in 1907.

By now, the skilful winger had developed into a solid centre-half. Alongside him, Makepeace thrilled the fans with his fierce tackling and pin-point distribution. Makepeace was as famous a cricketer as he was a footballer, representing Lancashire and England along with his Goodison teammate Jack Sharp. Not surprisingly, the Blues were extremely proud of their talented all-rounders. Sharp was Everton's regular right winger for 11 years. He mixed speed with accuracy and strength and was once described as a 'pocket Her-cules'. On the cricket field, Sharp scored 105 for England against the Australians at The Oval. But his first love was Everton and he later became a director, as did his son, while running a famous sports shop in the Liverpool city centre.

Add to these stars, men like Jimmy Settle (a clinical finisher), Harold Hardman (a great Corinthian whose skills on the wing won him an Olympic Games soccer gold medal with Great Britain prior to him becoming one of the game's great administrators and later a Manchester United director for 50 years) and it is easy to see why Everton were amongst the great teams of the day.

And this is without mentioning the legendary Alex 'Sandy' Young. He sunk Newcastle United in the 1906 FA Cup Final and claimed crucial goals throughout his career, which brings us neatly back to 3 September 1906 and Everton's greatest First Division goals-coring feat against Manchester City.

Having mentioned that the Blues won this one-sided affair 9-1, I should now add that Young plundered four of the goals. The team were making their first appearance at Goodison following their April Cup triumph achieved in front of 75,000 people at the Crystal Palace. This, in itself, made it a special day.

The previous Saturday the side had opened the season with a 2-2 draw at Middlesbrough, a game which gave no indication of the goal blitz that was to come. The record books might suggest that City were always going to be on a hiding to nothing at Goodison against the supremely confident Cup holders. But the real reason for the goal rush could also have had something to do with the weather!

The Saturday had been the 'Glorious First' — the start of the partridge shooting season. It had coincided with the start of the football season with sportsmen shooting for goals, not game. To say there was a heatwave is an understatement. Temperatures in the mid-80s were reported throughout the country with Liverpool itself basking in 13 hours of sunshine and a high of 86 degrees.

Manchester City had entertained Woolwich Arsenal at Hyde Road (their home until 1923 when they moved to Maine Road). The heat was described in one report as being 'terrifying' and the end product was that City finished the afternoon with just six men on the pitch. Just as remarkable is the scoreline which reveals that The Arsenal won by only 4-1.

The City players seemed incapable of dealing with the hot-house conditions. They had eight men on the field when the second half started and the referee offered to stop the game. The Lon-

Two contrasting shots of Everton's 1906 FA Cup-winning team. One photograph is taken at Goodison Park, the other being a grander picture in front of a mock back-drop depicting the Crystal Palace, the Final venue. The names in the latter group are: Standing (left to right): Mr A.R.Taylor, H.Makepeace, Mr W.C.Cuff, A.Young, Mr J.Davies, Mr E.A.Bainbridge, J.D.Taylor, Mr G.Maon, W.Scott, Mr B.Kelly, Wm Balmer, Mr H.Wright, J.Elliott. Sitting: Mr W.R.Clayton, Dr J.C.Baxter, J.Sharp, H.Bolton, W.Abbott, J.Settle, J.Crelley, H.P.Hardman, Dr W.Whitford, Mr D.Kirkwood.

doners, two up at the time, politely declined the official's offer of an early cold bath. But it appears they held back on their struggling opponents and settled for the 4-1 winning margin. It was described as a novel and unique incident in the history of the First Division.

City now came to Goodison to face Young, Sharp, Balmer, and the rest. Whether they were still feeling the heat or whether they simply did not fancy the challenge is open to debate. It's enough to say they turned up and were promptly played off the park. The 'Liverpool Daily Post', reporting the game the following day, said: *The inglorious display of City against Woolwich on Saturday before their own supporters did not suggest a tough job for the Toffees at Goodison. The evening was fine and 10,000 spectators were there at the start. Makepeace was absent and Tom Booth substituted. The Blues worked with determination and, keeping the leather well in, gradually forced back the Mancunian defence.*

That 'old warhorse' Taylor was not just a steadying influence in defence, but also scored the first goal, shooting beyond 'keeper Davis who would finish the game totally shell-shocked. Settle beat him easily to make it 2-0 and the cheers had only just died down when a smart pass from Young to Settle produced goal number three.

Abbott scored the fourth after a brilliant interchange between Taylor, Wilson and Young. It was surprising that Young had not found the net himself, but he soon put that right when he met a Wilson corner-kick. It gave the home side a 5-0 interval lead and it seemed that Everton could stroll through the visiting defence at will.

A clever pass by Settle enabled Young to bag number six and the centre-forward then completed his hat-trick with a 'rattling good shot'. Amazingly, City pulled one back on the break as the light began to fade. Two minutes from time, Bolton made it 8-1 and Young made it a match to remember when he headed home Sharp's centre for a record-breaking 9-1 win. The record still stands and, like Dixie Dean's League scoring feat, is never likely to be beaten.

Everton: Scott, W.Balmer, Crelly, Booth, Taylor, Abbott, Sharp, Bolton, Young, Settle, G.Wilson.
Attendance: 16,000

Everton in 1909. Notice the high waste-band and familiar snake-belt of Sandy Young, the 1906 Cup Final hero. Back row (left to right): Harris, R.Balmer, Scott, Maconnachie, Taylor, Makepeace. Front: Sharp, Coleman, White, Young, Turner.

Last Gasp Champions On A Day Of High Drama

Monday, 26 April 1915

Everton 2 Chelsea 2

FEW teams have won the League Championship with as much character and grit as Everton's school of 1915. The Blues suffered a major set-back in the run-in when they lost successive home games to Burnley and Sheffield Wednesday.

The men from Goodison now had to go on their travels, facing four away games on the trot. They won every single one of them — against Sunderland, West Brom, Bradford and Manchester City — to power from fifth place to first with just one game left.

Everything would now be decided on the last day with Everton and Oldham Athletic side by side on 45 points. As fate would have it, the Latics were up against Liverpool at Boundary Park. The Evertonians could not decide if this was a good thing or a bad thing as they prepared for their final game against Chelsea.

As it turned out, the Reds from across Stanley Park turned out to be the most reliable of neighbours. Their battling victory over Oldham and Everton's 2-2 home draw with Chelsea meant that the title trophy would reside in the board room at Goodison Park for only the second time since the inception of the League in 1888. Remarkably, the Blues were given a very low-key write-up in the local Press based on the fact that Chelsea were down amongst the First Division dead men and should have been crushed rather than held.

Certainly, the Blues were penned in for long periods in the early stages, possibly feeling the pressure after their long spell on 'tour' which had produced eight vital points out of eight. Strangely, they had been given a somewhat muted reception from the fans when they took

Joe Clennell, a free-scoring inside-forward, figured in 36 League games during the 1915 title run, scoring 14 goals.

to the field, Chelsea possibly getting a louder cheer.

It was only when the Blues became fiery on the field that the supporters responded to their cause. It was Tom Fleetwood, an attacking wing-half, who stirred things up with a zig-zag run and a low cross shot that found the net to make it 1-0. Now Everton's leading scorer Bobby Parker took centre-stage with an outstanding strike to make it 2-0.

Parker had been signed from Glasgow Rangers in November 1913 and finished off that season with 17 goals in 24 League games. This latest offering took his 1914-15 tally to 36 in 35 games which made him the First Division's leading scorer.

It was a classic effort, a goal worthy of winning any Championship. Harrison powered in corner and Parker drew back his boot, flashing a hook shot high

49

into the roof of the net to inspire a standing ovation from all corners of the ground.

Incredibly, the Blues lived on their nerves in a tense finale and Brittain pulled one back before Logan equalised with a penalty. Thanks to Liverpool's triumph at Oldham, the point was good enough to secure the Championship. Everton finished on 46 with the Latics on 45. It had been a long and tense campaign, but no one at Goodison was complaining.

Everton: Fern; Thompson, Weller, Fleetwood, Galt, Grenyer, Chedgzoy, Kirsopp, Parker, Clennell, Harrison.
Attendance: 30,000

Ten Thousand Holes In Blackburn Lancashire's Defence!

Saturday, 4 January 1919

Everton 9 Blackburn Rovers 0

FOOTBALL was played on a regional basis during World War One. Everton played in the Lancashire Section Principal Tournament which they won in season 1918-19, suffering only one defeat (at Manchester City) in 30 matches. The Blues subsequently lost to Midland Section winners Nottingham Forest in a two-legged Championship decider before finishing the campaign in the Lancashire Subsidiary Tournament.

Alan Grenyer was a left-half who played his best football for the Blues during World War One.

The highlight of the year was undoubtedly a 9-0 thrashing of Blackburn Rovers at Goodison Park. It does not stand as a record of any sort because of its county status, but it is still worth recording, if only for the five-goal blast from centre-forward Billy Gault.

It was reported that the ground was sticky and that there were 'pranks and miskicks aplenty', although it would appear that most of the action occured in the Rovers penalty area. Early in the match, the Blues were criticised for producing very little at the end of graceful combined movements. Some-one even commented that the shooting was not what you might call deadly.

It was as if the team picked up on these jibes because they opened the scoring after 15 minutes and then proceeded to swamp their opponents with an avalanche of attacks and goals.

Gault was the first on the mark, driving the ball low and wide of Gaskell's left hand and Everton soon increased their lead with an effort that was poetically described as a 'Miller thriller, a goal in a thousand'. The skilful right winger took the ball along the flank, beating the half-back and then the full-back before veering infield and hammering home a terrific low shot.

Rovers were being outclassed in all departments and Gault snatched the third after the 'keeper mishandled. On the half-hour a Joe Clennell header crashed into the back of the net to make it 4-0. The inside-left was all smiles, having joined the Blues from Blackburn in 1914. Clennell had been a virtual ever-present in the 1914-15 Championship-winning side. In wartime football he managed to amass 114 goals in only 104 games and this effort against his old club was a typical opportunist effort.

Clennell would make it 5-0 early in

the second half, netting from close range after a solo run. Then Gault took a centre from left winger Joe Donnachie to bring the total to 6-0 with the light fading fast over Goodison Park. Donnachie's far-post centre was his speciality. He was a real crowd favourite with his jinking runs and is one of that elite band of individuals who enjoyed two spells at Goodison Park.

The Blues now dropped down a gear, one report suggesting they were 'fiddling around a lot, plainly refusing to rub salt into Blackburn's wounds'. In truth, the players were just catching their breath before producing a storming finish with Gault unstoppable. He made it 7-0 with a low shot and 8-0 with a cheeky backheel which meant he had claimed a traditional hat-trick and five goals in all. Wareing scored the ninth and the crowd were still shouting for more. Clearly, there had been a fresh delivery of salt!

Everton: Mitchell; Thompson, Maconnachie, Fleetwood, Wareing, Grenyer, Miller, Jefferis, Gault, Clennell, Donnachie.
Attendance: 8,000

Left: Frank Jefferis helped to demolish Blackburn Rovers 9-0 in a Lancashire Section clash in 1919. Jefferis was a scheming inside-forward and a top-class tactician.

Right: John Maconnachie was a highly polished left-back from Scotland, showing skill at a time when most defenders opted for the long punt downfield. He starred against Blackburn in that 1919 massacre at Goodison.

The famous Sammy
Chedgzoy, who was
an established wing
star when Dixie
Dean made his home
debut against Villa.
Chegzoy had won a
League
Championship medal
in 1915 and was
responsible for a
revolutionary change
to the offside law.

Dixie Signs In For A Goal-Den Future

Saturday, 28 March 1925

Everton 2 Aston Villa 0

TRANSFER speculation was rife around Goodison Park as the 1924-25 season, a disappointing one for Everton, entered the home straight. In mid-March the 'Liverpool Echo' reported that the Blues were on the verge of making some bold moves with a view to rebuilding the team. Many people were asking why they did not move locally for talent with the main topic of conversation surrounding Tranmere's talented teenage striker Dixie Dean.

The 'Echo's' respected columnist, one 'Bee' (Ernest Edwards), was quick to point out that many clubs had been testing the water at Prenton Park and that *the time is ripe for the transfer of the boy.*

Edwards added: *Price is everything and Tranmere won't part with such a money-producer for a mere song. He ought not to go far from our doors, seeing that to all extents and purposes he is a local. He is, to my mind, the most promising centre-forward I have seen for years.*

The following morning, Tuesday, 17 March 1925, the 'Liverpool Daily Post' was able to report that the Blues had scooped the likes of Manchester United, Aston Villa, Albion, Birmingham, Huddersfield, Liverpool, Middlesbrough, Chelsea and a host of other clubs to sign Dean.

The 18-year-old centre-forward had plundered 27 goals in 27 games for Rovers, who were reported to have put a £2,500 price tag on his head as well as seeking a gift of other players from the club securing his signature. The 'Post' said: *It is probably the heaviest transfer fee that has ever been paid for a mere boy. It is impossible to state the figure with any degree of accuracy, but*

we can state definitely that £2,500 was Tranmere's original claim for their treasure.

The paper then made a personal plea to the Evertonians, saying: *Everton once had another boy on their books who started well, but eventually fell through the fraility of human nature and the sickly adulation of the crowd. It is to be hoped the crowd will not make a 'god' of Dean. He is very human and has many boy-like touches. It is not so much what he has done but the way he has done it. He is a natural footballer with a stout heart, a willing pair of feet and a constitution that will stand him in good stead.*

'Bee' picked up on the debate in the 'Echo' in typically humorous fashion, writing an imaginary postcard from the 'Echo Hive, 17 March 1925'. It said: *Dear spectator. Pardon my intrusion, but you may have heard that Dixie Dean has been transferred by Tranmere Rovers to Everton. It is not a world-making move; it is just the movement of a local boy from Prenton Park to Goodison Park. At Tranmere there has been too much talk of Dixie-this and Dixie-that. If it continues, the boy — he is but eighteen years old — may easily lose his balance and his football form. Do not imagine that I am intruding or that I am not not going to take a firm hold on my own writings about the boy. Do be normal — and let him be likewise.*

The message was a simple one. Give Dean a chance to develop without undue pressure. As it turned out, there was no need for concern. The player remained the most level-headed individual in the game, even when he was at the very height of his success and scoring goals hand over fist for Everton and England.

Young Dixie made his Everton debut at Arsenal on 21 March 1925, a 3-1 losing experience. Seven days later he was selected for the home game against Aston Villa. The 'Echo' reported: *It is*

The young Dixie Dean loved every minute of his exciting new challenge with Everton. Here he shares a joke with defender Tom Griffiths, who joined the Blues in 1926-27.

as plain as daylight that Everton are going to sweep away the tradition of a year ago and aim at young men with a push and go that has been missing from some of the ranks of the side. Everton have been very pretty; they have been tantalisingly so. Now the club directors have shown a firm hand, and are in effect stating that the side has not nearly been good enough and must be amended. The new Everton shall be forceful and enterprising.

And so Villa came to Goodison Park, the bridesmaids at Dean's wedding. The young man with a glorious future ahead of him was soon into his stride, getting in a snap shot after Smart had mis-kicked. The ball struck the goalkeeper's body and spun across goal with Talbot dashing in to clear. But Dixie's dream of making it a Goodison scoring debut was realised when his partner Kennedy bamboozled the Villa defence into thinking he was going to allow a forward ball to run out for a corner. Instead, he hooked a centre-back to Dean, who hammered it into the back of the net. The crowd gave their new hero a standing ovation.

In the second half, Dean began to direct headers wide to both flanks, giving the wingers the kind of service that would be his hallmark in years to come. He was always looking for openings around the box and directed an Alec Troup centre just over the top. Late on, another Troup cross, this time from a corner, was drilled home by left-half Reid to make it 2-0. It was very much the start of a new Goodison era.

Everton: Harland; McDonald, O'Donnell, Brown, McBain, Reid, Chedgzoy, Irvine, Dean, Kennedy, Troup.

Attendance: 25,000

Dean's First Goodison Treble

Saturday, 24 October 1925

Everton 4 Leeds United 2

IN A memorable Everton career, Dixie Dean would score many hat-tricks for the Blues. His first came at Burnley on 17 October 1924. His first Goodison treble arrived the following Saturday when Leeds United came to town.

It took Dean just three minutes to find the mark, a fine shot cannoning into the back of the net off an upright. Dean's anticipation of the early forward ball served him well and the 28,000 crowd showed their appreciation. There was an amazing scramble on the Leeds goal-line soon afterwards with the ball trapped under several players until goalkeeper Johnson somehow managed to clear, but it was not long before Dean increased the lead with an unusual goal.

Sam Chedgzoy got away down the flank and hoisted the ball into the centre. Dean came charging forward and although he was hampered by the close attentions of a defender, he somehow managed to head the ball into the corner of the net.

Chedgzoy was possibly Everton's best forward at this stage with his spurting runs and effective centres. The Blues, though, failed to cash in until the 37th minute when Kennedy netted with a first-time drive following more outstanding work by the winger.

The 3-0 interval lead was well deserved, but Leeds were not going to give in without a fight. Centre-forward Jennings rattled the woodwork with Menham well beaten, but Dean responded by making it 4-0 after 55 minutes, thus completing his first home treble for the Blues. It wasn't a hat-trick in the old-fashioned sense (three successive goals) but it was still an achievement the young man from Birkenhead could be extremely proud of and the crowd gave him a rousing cheer. Once again, Chedgzoy was the provider. Dean got a foot to the centre and the ball

Tiny Scottish winger Alec Troup, who had previously played for Forfar Athletic and Dundee, was the man who helped Dean to many of his 377 goals for the Blues. Troup wasn't on the scoresheet against Leeds, but he had another good game, causing opposing defenders all sorts of trouble.

dropped just under the bar with the 'keeper nowhere.

Wainscott pulled one back for Leeds after 63 minutes, but a minute later he was badly injured and taken to hospital with a dislocated elbow.

The ten men now battled gamely and Jennings reduced the lead still further with a fine drive a minute from time. But the day belonged to Dean as so many others would in the future. In the space of two weeks he had bagged six goals to suggest that glorious days were ahead in a blue shirt.

Everton: Menham; McDonald, Livingstone, Brown, Bain, Hart, Chedgzoy, Peacock, Dean, Kennedy, Troup.
Attendance: 28,660

A Goodison Christmas Cracker

25 December 1926

Everton 5 Sunderland 4

EVERTON had not won for six weeks when they entertained Sunderland on Christmas Day 1926. They were desperate for a holiday victory and secured it in the most dramatic of circumstances, winning at Goodison Park by the odd goal in nine.

Dixie Dean, playing his tenth game after recovering from a nightmare motor-cycle accident, was the undisputed hero of the day with an outstanding four-goal haul. But elsewhere another famous centre-forward, Middlesbrough's George Camsell, was bettering Dean's achievement by scoring five against Manchester City at Maine Road.

Head and shoulders above the rest, as usual, Dixie Dean rises above another frustrated 'keeper to power a header on target.

Camsell would go on to claim 59 League goals and set a new Football League scoring record. Dean would take note and do something about it 12 months on, but for now it was all about a crucial win over the men from Roker which finally brought to an end a worrying barren spell.

The Blues had lost 5-1 to Burnley, 1-0 to Cardiff, 5-3 to Aston Villa, drawn 1-1 with Bolton, thanks to an own-goal, and lost 2-1 at Manchester United. There were those who said relegation was not so much a possibility as a certainty. The Everton players now gave the fans the perfect Christmas present.

Over 37,000 turned up for the clash, the biggest Christmas attendance at Goodison for years. A young man by the name of Ted Critchley, signed from Stockport for a nominal fee, was handed his debut. It was hoped he would eventually prove an admirable replace-ment for famous right-winger Sammy Chedgzoy, the man who had been responsible for a major change to the offside law.

Chedgzoy had recognised a glaring loophole in the laws and exploited it in a game against Tottenham, dribbling the ball in along the by-line and then hammering it into the net without any other player touching it. Twelve months later, the football authorities were forced to introduce a new rule whereby the taker of a corner could play the ball only once before a second player had touched it.

Chedgzoy had retired at the end of the 1925-6 season, crossing the Atlantic to live in America. It meant the number seven shirt he had worn over a period of some 15 years was up for grabs and men like Irvine, Parker, Moffatt, Mil-lington and Woodhouse had all worn it that season before Critchley stepped

Dixie Dean the family man, taking a golfing break in the Isle of Man.

into the frame on Christmas Day. The 'Liverpool Echo' reported: *The Stockport boy did well. His one run the full length of the field was something to memorise, but allowing for his over-anxiety, which made him run the ball out, his old mannerisms and passes and centres augers well for future days.*

Those words proved prophetic. Critchley, with his tight control and speed, would provide teammate Dean with countless goals and serve the club well for eight years. Dixie rattled in four against Sunderland, but the best goal of the day was scored by inside-forward Bobby Irvine, who was a magnificent dribbler. He lashed home an outstanding first-time drive in an end-to-end affair that finished 5-4 in Everton's favour with Sunderland more than playing their part.

Everton: Davies; Raitt, O'Donnell, Brown, Bain, Hart, Critchley, Irvine, Dean, Dominy, Troup.
Attendance: 37,500

One Down, Fifty-Nine To Go

Saturday, 27 August 1927

Everton 4 Sheffield Wednesday 0

THE dawning of the 1927-28 season was a significant one for Everton. The previous year, star striker Dixie Dean had been badly injured in a summer motor accident in which he fractured his skull. His durability was such that he was pulling on his famous number nine shirt just four and a half months later and scoring in an August fixture at Leeds.

Dean went on to claim 21 League goals in 27 games with three in the Cup for good measure. It was as if the accident had sharpened his appetite for big-match action rather than dulled it and so when the new campaign kicked-off with a home clash against Sheffield Wednesday, there was tremendous anticipation amongst the Evertonians

that the season would hold something very special indeed.

It turned out to be a record-breaking year in every sense, a goal-packed Championship charge in which Dixie would find the back of the net 60 times on League duty to claim a VIP place in the Goodison Park Hall of Fame.

The first of those goals came against Wednesday on a day when new captain Warney Cresswell led the team out for the very first time. The pitch was in perfect condition and while Cresswell lost the toss, it mattered little because there was no bright sunshine or wind to give an advantage.

The Blues almost scored in the opening 60 seconds when Alec Troup lobbed the ball into the area. It seemed too high to kick and too low to head, but Dixie made the most of it with a magnificent dive that very nearly produced a headed goal.

Albert Virr, a no-nonsense half-back who was prominent against Sheffield Wednesday the day Dixie Dean scored against Sheffield Wednesday to begin his push for the legendary '60'.

Factfile: On the day of this victory, it was revealed that Everton had made the heaviest financial loss in the First Division the previous season as they invested heavily in the transfer market in a successful battle to avoid relegation. It was stated that for every club that lost money, there were three who made a profit. Three Lancashire clubs failed to cover their expenditure with their income — Blackburn, Bury and Everton.

Everton's first-time football was a treat to watch. The ball flashed from one man to the other to leave Wednesday gasping. It was no surprise when the lead was claimed after 26 minutes. Winger Troup was the scorer, squeezing home a shot from what had seemed an impossible angle to startle goalkeeper Brown. The lead was increased within a minute when inside-left Weldon hammered home from long range. At the other end, Everton's solid Scottish centre-back Hunter Hart ensured that opposing centre-forward Jimmy Trotter didn't get in a single shot.

At the start of the second half, the Blues began to pepper the Wednesday goal as Dean, Forshaw and Virr all went close. Forshaw made it 3-0 after 62 minutes, Dean heading into his path after O'Donnell had launched the ball in. The victory was completed when Dean took Irvine's well-timed pass on the run and slipped his shot wide of the helpless Brown.

For the Goodison number nine it was a case of one down, 59 to go. George Camsell's League scoring record was clearly in his sights.

Everton: Taylor, Cresswell, O'Donnell, Kelly, Hart, Virr, Irvine, Forshaw, Dean, Weldon, Troup.

Attendance: 39,485

Dean now went from the sublime to the ridiculous. The referee stunned everyone by ignoring Wednesday's bold offside appeals and Cresswell was allowed to break forward and slide an inch-perfect pass into the box. It seemed as if Dean could not miss in front of the posts, but he pulled his shot wide and the visitors couldn't believe their luck. Stirred by this miss, the centre-forward then bulleted a header against the bar.

Dixie Dean's Finest Hour

Saturday, 5 May 1928

Everton 3 Arsenal 3

IF there was such a thing as a soccer time machine and Evertonians were offered just one magical trip into the past, I suggest that they would opt, to a man, to be whisked back to Goodison Park on Saturday, 5 May 1928 to witness William Ralph 'Dixie' Dean's finest hour.

The League Championship had already been won. Now the greatest number nine the game has ever seen was standing on the brink of immortality with George Camsell's Football League scoring record of 59 goals locked in his sights.

Could Dean rewrite the record books by equalling and possibly beating the Middlesbrough striker's formidable tally? The challenge against the mighty Arsenal was all too clear. Dean needed three goals to become a record-breaker. For most strikers, the task would be a mountainous one. But Dixie was no ordinary player. Here was the complete footballer, fast and powerful, possessing a lethal shot in both feet and the undisputed king of the air.

There was a genuine sense of history in the making as thousands of fans converged on Goodison Park in bright sunshine. It was as if the gods themselves wanted to be part of football's greatest day.

Incidentally, most reports give a crowd figure of 60,000 for this match, but the official figure returned to the Football League was just over 48,000. Years later, half of Merseyside would claim to have been present on this historic day.

Arsenal were never going to be pushovers. One of their most successful players, Charlie Buchan, was playing in his final match before bowing out. The Gunners were not interested in Dean. They wanted to win it for Charlie. The game had so many aspects, not least the fact that the League Championship trophy was going to be presented on the final whistle.

Copying Wembley's lead, amplifiers had been spread around Goodison so that every fan in the ground would be able to hear League president John

A proud Championship group pose in May 1928 with the Gwladys Street terraces behind them. Notice there is no stand. The houses are clearly visible. From the left: Harry Cooke, Critchley, Martin, Kelly, Cresswell (captain), O'Donnell, Mr W.C.Cuff (chairman), Hart, Dean, Davies, Weldon, Virr and Troup.

64

McKenna during the post-match celebrations. The fans had been encouraged in the local Press to keep off the pitch at all times. All they had to do was cheer Everton and Dean in particular every inch of the way.

Reflecting on the big match, the 'Liverpool Echo' reported: *In many clubs, success such as one man (Dean) has won would have been fatal. There would have been petty jealousies, but at Everton that is not the case. They all recognise Dean's worth and his great help, and naturally they are as keen as Dean to see Camsell's record go by.*

A new entrance from Bullens Road had been created for the first time, from which the mounted police could be brought into the ground at any given moment, if required. The trophy was already on display and a supporter shouted to the Goodison officials: "Where are the colours?" The hint was taken and secretary Tom McIntosh immediately tied royal blue ribbons to the trophy. This was a day for single-minded bias.

Chairman Will Cuff opened the proceedings by urging the crowd to remain in the places on the final whistle. Then there was a sensational Goodison welcome for skipper Warney Cresswell as he led out the team. The warmth of the supporters also touched Buchan as he emerged from the tunnel, wearing an Arsenal shirt for the last time.

Referee Mr W.P.Harper of Stourbridge took the unusual step of giving Dean a hearty handshake. And all eyes were on the centre-circle as the official finally got the proceedings underway. Carried forward on the crest of an almighty roar, Dean had an early chance, but did not score.

The Arsenal now attacked themselves and snatched the lead dramatically with just two minutes on the clock. Shaw appeared to handle as he moved through, but he got away with it and his shot went straight through the 'keeper's hands into the back of the net. The match was clearly not going to script and the fans were temporarily stunned, but the man of the moment now responded with a quite sensational

double with the game only three minutes old!

The crowd went absolutely wild when a Ted Critchley corner was turned on by George Martin to Dean. The centre-forward sent a header into the extreme left-hand corner of the net and it was 1-1. The ground now rocked as tens of thousands of voices picked up on the moment with Dean closing in on goal for a second time. Long-legged centre-half Butler ran across him and the Everton ace crashed to the ground. The cry of 'Penalty'! was so loud, it rattled the slates on a thousand and one houses in the surrounding streets.

The referee immediately pointed to the spot and Dean got up, placed the ball himself and drilled it wide of Bill Paterson to equal Camsell's 59 goal record (the Middlesbrough player had achieved his feat in the Second Division).

The prince of goalscorers now needed just one more to be king. At the same time, Everton were nearing the 104 goals record total achieved by West Brom shortly after World War One. The Blues' total was 101 and the statisticians in the crowd were beginning to think about a possible team record as well as an individual achievement. After all, the game still had 87 minutes to run.

At the same time, the play was enthralling. Paterson claimed a hot-shot from Dean who was now pumped up to fever pitch. The big attacker followed in with a shoulder charge that nearly sent the 'keeper sprawling into the back of the net. The crowd would have been happy to see Dixie pick up the Arsenal custodian and throw him over the line, ball and all.

The Gunners had already beaten Everton twice at Highbury, 3-2 on Christmas Eve and 4-3 in the fourth round of the FA Cup. The Blues were now intent on a very special revenge, but Buchan and Shaw demonstrated their artistry to indicate that the match would be fiercely contested to the finish.

In his anxiety to get the record, Dean began to fall into Arsenal's offside trap. Everton's frustration reached new heights when the Londoners equalised

If Dean was blasting home goals, he was pitching for glory in other areas. He enjoyed a game of baseball and won honours playing for local club Caledonians. Everton secured his baseball medal at a Glasgow auction in October 1991, along with his 1931-32 Championship medal and other key items of memorablia.

The most important goal ever scored at Goodison? Dixie Dean pounces to claim his record-breaking 60th in the League game against Arsenal in 1928.

The most important goal ever scored at Goodison? Dixie Dean pounces to claim his record-breaking 60th in the League game against Arsenal in 1928.

ten minutes before the interval. Goalkeeper Davies was about to pick the ball up when left-back O'Donnell contrived to turn it over his own line to make it 2-2. It had been a pulsating opening 45 minutes and the players and the fans were grateful for the half-time whistle and an opportunity to catch their breath.

On the resumption, the tension was unbearable. Paterson made an outstanding save as Dean got full power on a wickedly spinning ball. He now showed the other side of his game, slipping a neat pass to Critchley, who hammered a shot against the angle of the post. Everton had the sun in their eyes and were almost certainly trying too hard, but such frantic play was inevitable with so much at stake. Dean now found himself crowded out for a spell, but he broke through with power on the hour to swing a shot narrowly wide.

The minutes were now ticking away. Dean headed inches over and then over-ran the ball on the break. He sent a left-foot shot wide and as the game went into the final ten minutes, hope was turning to despair. But Dixie was the man for all occasions and he seemed to grow visibly when the Blues gained a corner-kick after Paterson had punched Martin's shot over the bar.

Tiny Scottish winger Alec Troup, the man who had provided most of the ammunition for Dean throughout that famous year, now hoisted the ball high into the box. Dean rose out of a ruck of players to head home with all the power and accuracy that was his trademark.

The 60-goal haul that many felt was impossible had been achieved and the centre-forward was congratulated by all of his team mates. Two spectators broke through the police barrier and one was bundled off by the referee. The other managed to reach his hero and give him a kiss! Goalkeeper Paterson took off his cap and scratched his head, accepting that he had been beaten three times by the master.

There were still eight minutes left and during this closing spell the crowd never stopped cheering for a single second, even when Arsenal centre-forward Shaw levelled matters on the rebound after Davies had turned a Peel effort against the upright. As Everton shaped to take a corner at the other end. the Gunners' goalkeeper Paterson took the opportunity to shake hands with Dean. And even while the kick was being taken, centre-half Butler was seen to shake hands with the man who had given him such a torrid afternoon.

Suddenly it was all over. Cresswell stepped up to receive the Championship trophy from Mr McKenna. Everton's famous chairman Cuff tried to make himself heard over the loudspeakers, congratulating the team on their title success, adding that it had been the most wonderful season the game of football had ever known.

The toast was Everton Football Club and Dixie Dean . . .the greatest centre-forward of all time.

Everton: Davies; Cresswell, O'Donnell, Kelly, Hart, Virr, Critchley, Martin, Dean, Weldon, Troup.
Attendance: 48,715.

Famous 'Liverpool Echo' cartoonist George Green saluted Dean's 60-goal League haul with an extra-special drawing. The fans loved it.

Another historic George Green cartoon hails the 1928 Champions. It was hats off to Everton.

Sagar Begins His Goodison Marathon

18 January 1930

Everton 4 Derby County 0

TED Sagar was the Goodison Park marathon man. He spent an astonishing 24 years and one month with the Blues between 1929 and 1953 to set up a club record of 463 League appearances (some record books give the uncorrect figure of 465). The goalkeeper who became an Everton legend first appeared on the scene on 18 January 1930, named in place of the experienced Davies. As a boy, he had played for Thorne Colliery in the Doncaster Senior League and was on the verge of signing for Hull City when Everton nipped in smartly to secure his services.

The fans turned up for the County clash, fascinated by the debut appearance of the young 'keeper who had been earning himself good reports with the Reserves. He soon demonstrated a safe pair of hands, claiming a shot-cum-centre from Bobby Barclay. This apart, there was very little for the young Sagar to do. Ted Critchley secured the lead after 22 minutes with a well-placed side-foot shot. Derby now made what was only their second attack of note and once again Sagar was equal to a high forward ball.

The initiative remained with the Blues although their new 'keeper earned applause when he dashed out to collect a ball that Harry Bedford had headed in. Dean made it 2-0 after 51 minutes after Derby 'keeper Harry Wilkes had failed to hold a fiery shot from Jimmy Stein.

Sagar now showed the bravery that would become one of his hallmarks, plunging down at the feet of Bedford. His other strength was his confidence going for crosses and he leapt to make a good catch after George Mee had centred across the goalmouth.

Soon after, he punched away in similar circumstances and the 'Football Echo' reported: *Sagar had undoubtedly justified his inclusion, although it was Everton's teamwork which had gained the day.*

The Blues went three up after 75 minutes, Dean having the simple task of guiding the ball in with his body after Wilkes had failed to claim a Stein centre. Three minutes from time, Stein's hot drive made it 4-0. It had been a successful debut for Sagar, but he now stepped down for three games to allow Davies to return.

Sadly, things were now deteriorating for the Blues in terms of all-round results. Sagar was able to get a seven-match run, but relegation-haunted Everton lost five of these matches and conceded 19 goals in the bargain.

The young 'keeper's confidence might have been destroyed when Billy Coggins, signed from Bristol City, now claimed the first-team jersey for the remainder of a frustrating relegation season. More than that, Coggins was an ever-present the following year as the Blues swept back to the top flight at the first time of asking.

But Sagar's quality was such that he was the man in the driving seat when a bright new First Division challenge loomed on 29 August 1931. The supremely talented goalkeeper never looked back.

He won two League Championship medals and an FA Cup winners' medal with the Blues and finished up with a marvellous total of 495 League and Cup games under his slim belt. He had many memorable moments, but that debut clean sheet against Derby County always gave him particular pleasure.

Everton: Sagar; Williams, O'Donnell, Robson, Hart, McPherson, Critchley, Martin, Dean, Rigby, Stein.

Attendance: 35,436

Ted Sagar is an Everton legend. He played in 495 games for the Blues, making his debut in 1930 and turning out for the last time in 1952. He had superb judgement and his ability earned him two Championship medals and an FA Cup winners' medal. Sagar is pictured in action against Sunderland.

Relegated After A Storming Victory!

Saturday, 3 May 1930

Everton 4 Sunderland 1

A DISASTROUS six-game losing spell between 5 March and 12 April had left Everton in a precarious position as the 1929-30 season reached a nail-biting climax. Aston Villa, Newcastle United, West Ham, Birmingham, Leicester and Grimsby Town had all overshadowed the Blues in a disappointing spell and now Dixie Dean, scorer of 109 League goals in a richly productive three-year spell, was suddenly unavailable for selection.

It was doom and gloom at Goodison Park, but the side had shown its fighting qualities, embarking on a four-match unbeaten run (three victories and a draw) that had brought the Blues to the final game with a mathematical chance of staying up. Sadly, Everton's fate would depend on results other than their own.

All they could do was produce the goods against Sunderland at Goodison and keep their fingers crossed. Not surprisingly, the game attracted the club's biggest gate of the season with over 51,000 people in attendance. It was a sultry, humid afternoon and the Everton players were looking distinctly nervous as play got underway.

Warney Cresswell made a couple of uncharacteristic mistakes for such an old warrior and it served to unsettle the crowd. But the tension eased after 23 minutes when inside-left Tommy Johnson cashed in following a free-kick. Goalkeeper Robinson had punched away off Tommy White's head. There was something of a scramble until Johnson claimed the loose ball with the fans screaming for a shot. It was a long time in coming, but when it did, it flew home with the scorer mobbed by his delighted teammates.

Everton's elation lasted just six minutes. After some loose play in front of goal, Clunas arrived with a first-time drive to equalise. The supporters groaned in disappointment, but their frustration was shortlived because the Blues regained the lead almost immediately with a magnificent goal from

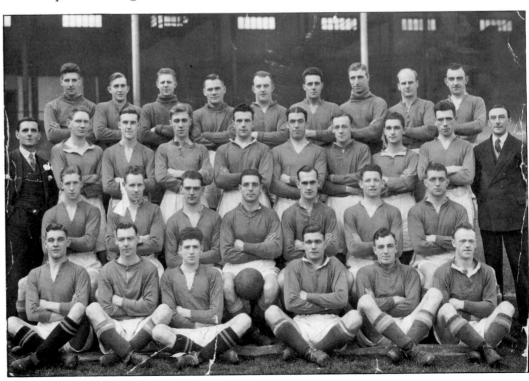

This 1929-30 squad of players had the misfortune of taking the club down for the first time, although they bounced back at the first time of asking. Back row (left to right): Thompson, Bryan, Sagar, O'Donnell, White, Martin, Coggins, Cresswell, Hart. Centre: Cooke (trainer), G.Cook, Webster, Britton, Gee, Dean, Common, Stein, Tucker, Robson. Below Centre: Wilkinson, McClure, Critchley, Williams, Griffiths, McCambridge, Johnson. Front: Low, Rigby, Chedgzoy, junior, Towers, McPherson, Dunn.

White. He met a lobbed centre and headed the ball downwards. Robinson managed to parry the effort, but White had followed in and he netted with a deft touch of his boot.

Everton went in with a 2-1 interval lead and all eyes immediately focussed on the score-board, an ABC guide to the goings on elsewhere. There was a huge sigh when the Burnley score went up because it showed them winning 1-0. But Grimsby and Newcastle had failed to score and so there was still some hope.

The home players responded by making it 3-1 after 65 minutes. White was the scorer after Ted Critchley, George Martin and Johnson had all tried their luck in a packed area. Sunderland now lost Lawley through injury and it helped Everton's cause.

White did well shrugging off the powerful Shaw before firing home a great goal for his hat-trick. The giant crowd were now waiting on news from elsewhere. Would Everton be relegated after three successive victories? There was a strange hush around the famous ground and then total despair when it was revealed the Blues would be going down.

The 'Football Echo' summed up the agony in a page one leader. It said: *Everton relegated! There is a sad ring about the words. Everton stood for the real football. Throughout forty-two years of League football, they have carried millions of people to heights of admiration uncommon for all but a few fortunate clubs. Of those millions, a tolerable minority will accept that even a classic club like Everton must go the way of the world and be relegated to Division Two. Their regret is ours. A noteworthy record has been broken.*

Since 1906-07 it has been the boast of three clubs — Everton, Aston Villa and Blackburn Rovers — that they alone of the original twelve clubs in the League had not been relegated to Division Two. It was Everton's particular boast that, of those three, they alone had not been helped out of relegation by voting in or extension of the League. Derby County were the previous club of the original 12 to break

their connection in Division One in 1907. Everton have withstood the strain for an additional 19 seasons, but now leave Villa and Rovers to share the record that was theirs. Sunderland's unbroken run dates only from 1891.

Billy Coggins, the man Ted Sagar eventually replaced, played in every game when Everton claimed the Second Division title in 1931. But Sagar soon claimed the jersey and Coggins moved to Queen's Park Rangers and Bath City before retiring to his native Bristol.

Everton had flirted dangerously with the big drop in 1922 and 1927 when they finished third from bottom. Now the unthinkable had finally happened. The 'Echo' then listed the order in which the ten 'originals', were relegated: Stoke 1890, Accrington and Notts County 1893, Burnley 1897, Bolton 1899, Preston and West Brom 1901, Wolves 1906, Derby 1907 and now Everton 1930.

The report concluded: *Those League derby days at Goodison Park and Anfield leave fond memories. It depends upon Everton how soon they are resumed.*

Everton: Coggins; Cresswell, O'Donnell, McPherson, Griffiths, Thomson, Critchley, Martin, White, Johnson, Rigby.

Attendance: 51,132

A Whole New Second Division Experience

3 September 1930

Everton 2 Preston North End 1

EVERTON, founder members of the Football League, were not relishing their very first home game in the Second Division on 3 September 1930. But at least they were in good company. Their Goodison Park opponents were Preston North End, who had won the very first Football League Championship back in 1888. The difference was that North End had been down since 1925, having also experienced the drop in 1901, 1912 and 1914. For the Blues it was a whole new experience and they were intent on getting back to the top flight at the earliest opportunity.

They had won on the opening day of the season at Plymouth Argyle and now the opportunity was there to take another step up the ladder on home soil. But while they secured a 2-1 success over the men from Deepdale, there were those in the crowd who were suggesting that, on this performance at least, the Blues would not go far in Division Two.

There was even criticism of Dixie Dean who failed to score for the second week running, but 'Liverpool Echo' correspondent Ernest Edwards took a very different tack. The forward line was ill-balanced, but he acquitted Dean of any blame, claiming it was the service and the support-play that was at fault.

Edwards wrote: *He went for every ball that was within hailing distance and his work with his head made him quite a force. Others may disagree with this view, but it is a considered opinion about a player who only had the ball passed to him on the turf but twice during the game. His heading is so deadly that I suppose I should not be critical of the perpetual height at which he had to take a 'pass', but I do say that his method is to present goals to those who should be at his side when they see him rise to the ball with his face towards his own goal. He can do no more than enlarge the position and create openings by his leap and header.*

In other words, Dean needed more support alongside him and a greater sense of anticipation from his attacking teammates. This was a day when the Blues relied on the class of defender Warney Cresswell and the control and

Stepping out at the start of the 1930-31 season, Everton's first-ever in Division Two, are George Martin, Tommy White, Dixie Dean, Billy Coggins and Tom Griffiths. The purposeful stride in a street near Goodison told its own story. Within eight months, the Blues would be back at the top.

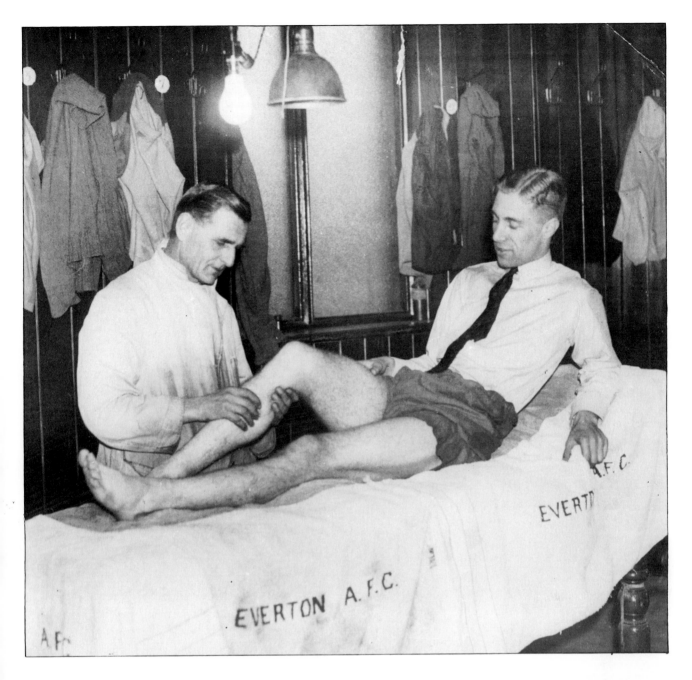

speed of Ted Critchley on the right wing.

Centre-half Tommy Griffiths was also influential, although this would be his last season in an Everton shirt. He would be injured halfway through the promotion campaign, lose his place to Charlie Gee and then be transferred to Bolton Wanderers. The Blues seemed to give Preston too much respect in the main. Tommy White failed to cash-in on a series of gift offerings from Dean's head. And the message from the fans was a simple one. Everton were being too easily brushed aside and hustled off the ball. The Second Division, it was said, would teach them a great lesson in this respect.

But while they were outpaced and outgeneralled, the home side still snatched the points. Griffiths opened the scoring from a lobbed centre by Cresswell. Harrison equalised with a scorching shot and White edged the Blues back in front.

The critics soon faded into the background as the Goodison outfit got their act together, opening with five straight wins. An intriguing campaign was gaining momentum with every passing week.

Everton: Coggins; Williams, Cresswell, McPherson, Griffiths, Thomson, Critchley, White, Dean, Martin, Rigby. *Attendance: 29,908*

Everton were determined to make their stay in the Second a short one. They opened up with five straight wins, getting off the mark at Goodison with a 2-1 win over Preston. A young Cliff Britton would soon make his bow an go on to become one of the most cultured wing-halves Everton have ever had. He is pictured receiving treatment from Harry Cooke.

Seven Goals Before Half-Time

Saturday, 28 February 1931

Everton 9 Southport 1

EVERTON'S total frustration at being relegated to the Second Division for the first time in their history proved to be a powerful motivating force in season 1930-31. The Blues produced a string of outstanding performances to link a memorable promotion campaign with a powerful FA Cup run.

Local rivals Southport, members of the Third Division North, provided the opposite in the quarter-finals and it turned out to be a record-breaking afternoon at Goodison with seven goals scored by the home side before half-time! The Seasiders were out-powered and out-classed on a mud-bath of a pitch. But it was snow that was the biggest worry to the fans on the morning of the game.

There was a severe fall, the likes of which had not been experienced all winter. Most people presumed the game would have to be postponed and yet, as if by a freak of nature, only the corners of the pitch were snow-capped with the middle area completely clear. Rumours were rife in the city that the tie might have to be abandoned because the snowflakes were so large, they might 'blind' the players and the referee. Yet

Everton scored a magnificent seven goals before half-time when beating local rivals Southport 9-1 in 1931 on a mudbath of a Goodison pitch. Dean scored four, including this spectacular header.

This heavily touched up picture almost has artistic merit. Dixie Dean appears to be hovering as he heads home his fourth and Everton's eighth against Southport in the 1931 Cup tie.

by 2pm, a large crowd had already gathered inside the ground, each and every one of them banking on a thrilling cup clash.

Plymouth, beaten earlier in the competition by the Blues, were generous enough to send a telegram to Goodison, wishing the home side well. Someone recalled that on the morning of the match in Plymouth, Everton had been greeted by a military band playing the 'Funeral March'. But their Cup dreams were still very much alive, even though Southport were promising them a rough ride with a lucrative semi-final place up for grabs.

The Evertonians shrugged aside all of this bold talk from their opponents. It was the Mayor of Southport's birthday and they were intent on making it an unhappy one, but the visitors arrived in considerable numbers, clearly identifiable Southport schoolboys with their maroon and black-striped caps and two young mascots, each wearing top hats. Everton wanted to win it for the skilful Ted Critchley, whose wife presented him with a daughter on the morning of the game.

Among those present was Mr John McKenna, the League president and Anfield stalwart who, in spite of the cold, climbed the giddy heights of the main grandstand to sit alongside Everton chairman Will Cuff. The pitch was in a dreadful state. The 'Football Echo' declared: *The Everton mud was in prime condition. At about 3.15pm it was high tide!*

Southport, anticipating being up to their ankles in it, had trained secretly on a ploughed field. The wags in the crowd suggested they could have borrowed Goodison. Four times, Everton captain Williams tossed the coin before the kick-off, only to see it stuck upright in the mud.

The visitors won the toss at the fifth

attempt and attacked the Stanley Park End. Southport advanced immediately down the left, but the ball appeared to turn into an oversized snowball as it rolled along the surface. The Blues claimed it and launched it forward, the opposing 'keeper completely misjudging the flight of the ball. Dean darted in behind him and ignored the presence of a full-back on the line, blasting home to make it 1-0.

The lead was increased after 12 minutes. It was Dunn who powered home after Dean had seen a shot kicked away. The Blues were in full flight and Dunn made it 3-0, once again inspired by Dean. Rather foolishly, the visitors now tried to use the offside trap against

Factfile: Everton lost 1-0 to West Brom at Old Trafford to miss out on Wembley. But as the next report reveals, promotion was now to be achieved at the first time of asking.

An unusual angle of Everton's ninth and final goal against Southport in 1931. The scorer is tricky inside-forward Tommy Johnson. Note the snow and mud which put the game in some considerable doubt. The fans are also standing under the Stanley Park Stand, an area which has been blocked off in recent years.

one of the liveliest forward lines in the business. Dean cashed in on a gift, set up by Johnson, and he completed his treble at the 35th-minute mark with a crack shot into the bottom right-hand corner. It was 5-0 and there was no sign of a let-up.

Critchley then gave his new baby a present by moving into the centre-forward position to claim goal number six after 37 minutes. Smiling broadly, the same player now celebrated in style with a pacy run that took him clear for what can only be described as 'The Magnificent Seven'.

The half-time whistle provided Southport with some much-needed respite and they staggered back to the dressing-room feeling distinctly shell-shocked. They actually managed to pull one back after the break, but the rampant Dean and his partner Johnson increased the lead to 9-1.

The visitors consoled themselves with a financial bonanza. Everton's ambitions stretched much further than the nearest bank. Wembley was now just one game away and it was a tantalising thought, even though promotion was priority number one. But for the time being, the mud-kings were happy with their emphatic quarter-final triumph.

Everton: Coggins; Williams, Cresswell, McClure, Gee, Thomson, Critchley, Dunn, Dean, Johnson, Stein.
Attendance: 45,647

Promoted
At The First Attempt

Saturday, 18 April 1931

Everton 3 Burnley 2

REVENGE and celebration were in the air as Everton prepared for their final home game of the 1930-31 season with League president John McKenna in the main stand, ready and willing to present the Second Division Championship shield.

Burnley had crushed the Blues 5-2 at Turf Moor in mid-December, Everton's heaviest defeat of the season. Now there was a wonderful opportunity to put that right while revelling in a title success. The crowd was not that big as the kick-off approached. It was estimated that around 18,000 were in the ground, but the inevitable late-comers would swell that number. There was a biting wind and a threat of rain, but a goal inside three minutes warmed the home fans. Johnson, a tricky inside-left who was the perfect foil for the powerful Dean, lashed home a powerful free-kick to make it 1-0.

The applause had hardly died away when Critchley conjured up one of the best goals seen on the ground for some time to increase the lead. Stein laid the foundations with a great centre when the ball had seemed certain to run out for a goal-kick. Dean tried to make contact with his head, but the ball sailed over him and Critchley reacted superbly, hooking home on the volley.

It would soon be three goals in nine minutes, but this time the opposition were celebrating. Shots cannoned away in a packed box until Beel found a way past Coggins from close range. Everton's two-goal advantage was restored when the unfortunate Wood conceded an own goal when trying to prevent Critchley's centre reaching Dean who was lying in wait.

Referee Kingscott had been selected to officiate at the FA Cup Final, but he struck a note of discord with the Evertonians.

Dean showed his annoyance at a particularly bad offside decision and the crowd reacted by booing the referee from all corners of the ground. The din continued for some time, but Dean helped to concentrate their thoughts with a superb pass to centre-half Gee, who had moved forward and only had the 'keeper to beat. Unfortunately, he shot like a defender, over the bar! It left the interval score at 3-1.

Mid-table Burnley had been outclassed, but Everton had not made the most of their chances. Priest reduced the arrears with a long-range shot that squeezed inside the post with Coggins at full stretch. But Everton retained a firm grip on the proceedings to finish winners on their special day.

Mr McKenna, presenting the shield to the Blues, said there was no reason why they should not go on and emulate Liverpool's feat of winning the Second and First Division titles in successive season. They were very prophetic words indeed.

Everton: Coggins; Williams, Cresswell, McClure, Gee, Thomson, Critchley, Martin, Dean, Johnson, Stein.
Attendance: 19,144

Charlie Gee, in the heart of the Everton defence when the Blues beat Burnley 3-2 to revel in their Second Division championship success in April 1931, he kept up the fine tradition of Goodison 'stoppers'.

Twelve Goals At Goodison In One Day

Saturday, 17 October 1931

Everton 9 Sheffield Wednesday 3

EVEN in the goal-mad 1930s, 12 goals in a single game was an attacking feast to be applauded by all and sundry. The irony of this sensational Goodison Park affair was that many fans were unable to fully appreciate the goal blitz because of the swirling fog that had threatened the match right up to kick-off time. There were many people outside the ground 15 minutes before the start, reluctant to venture through the gates for fear of a postponement.

It was not quite as bad as all that, but there was certainly enough fog about to make things difficult for the spectators. Visibility for the players was not too bad, but those fans at the back of the various stands were constantly straining when the ball was at its maximum distance away.

International calls robbed Wednesday of two key players, but their reserve strength was such that they still promised to be worthy opponents. But Everton were in rampant mood, having scored 15 goals in their five previous games. In the final reckoning, the Blues would be unstoppable with Dixie Dean in particular an irresistible force.

As Wednesday goalkeeper Brown picked the ball out of the back of the net for the ninth time, no doubt his mind went back to his non-League days when he had a similar experience against Spurs in the Cup while playing for Worksop Town.

Everton went ahead after 22 minutes when a neat back-header from Dean played Stein in. He thumped the ball wide of the 'keeper and the goal spree was on in earnest. The 'Football Echo' correspondent reflected on Dean's scoring prowess up to that stage of the season, suggesting that it had 'not been prolific'. The big centre-forward had managed 'only' two hat-tricks in the ten opening games! Dixie, always striving for that little bit extra in front of goal, would now respond with a magnificent five-goal haul.

He took a ball from defence, played a quick one-two with White and then hammered his shot home before Brown could move.

Wednesday pulled one back when Rimmer met a Burgess cross, heading wide of Sagar to make it 2-1. The half-time whistle came with the crowd unaware that the second period would be one long catalogue of outstanding goals.

Shell-shocked Wednesday would concede three in the space of ten minutes. White headed in after 46 minutes from a Critchley centre. Almost immediately, Stein took a bad knock as he moved past Beeson, but it did not prevent him from playing a sharp pass to Dean, who wheeled round and rifled a shot wide of the startled Brown to make it 4-1. The Sheffield outfit, weakened in defence, had no answer to the threat from Dean and a perfect header from Critchley's outstanding centre made it five with Dixie celebrating his third treble of the season.

Everton were dancing through the fog and Brown didn't know what hit him when he got in the way of a fierce shot from Dean. The superb Critchley now waltzed past two defenders before claiming goal number six on the hour.

Wednesday refused to give up the ghost and they pulled two back through Hooper and Ball to make it 6-3.

Dean responded at the double with goals in the 73rd and 75th minutes to complete his nap hand and Johnson, the man with the roving commission, finished off the visitors two minutes from time.

It was pointed out that Dean had scored five without getting a hat-trick which in those days was three on the run. We accept a hat-trick as a treble of any sort in the modern game, but they were more discerning in the past!

Dean would finish this Championship season with 45 goals in 38 League games, 15 short of his League record, but still a magnificent tally and one that emphasised his standing as the most dangerous striker in the land.

Everton: Sagar; Williams, Cresswell, Clark, Gee, Thomson, Critchley, White, Dean, Johnson, Stein.

Attendance: 38,186

Hail To Sunshine Dixie!

Saturday, 28 November 1931

Everton 9 Leicester City 2

EVERTON players were scoring hat-tricks as if they were going out of fashion as the 1931-32 season progressed towards what would be a Championship finale. Dunn had opened the campaign with a treble against Birmingham. White had followed up with three against Portsmouth.

Dean's personal satisfaction reached new heights when he rocked the old enemy at Anfield with an unforgettable hat-trick. The great man went on to plunder three at Sheffield United, five against Sheffield Wednesday, five against Chelsea and four in a 9-2 win over Leicester, the game featured here.

The weather had been unkind to the Blues, but the sun shone for the first time in weeks for the visit of the men from Filbert Street. The game opened with Everton employing their famous criss-cross passing movements, Johnson spraying the ball first to Critchley and then to Stein. Four men had a hand in Dean's opener after six minutes, the ball inevitably finding the net off the number nine's head.

Four minutes later the crowd roared once again when White increased the lead. Dean unselfishly played his teammate in and while the shot lacked power, it was still good enough to beat goal-keeper McLaren. It was not all one way and Sagar made saves from four different Leicester players before Everton went three up after 17 minutes.

It was again the result of the brilliant heading of Dean. When Critchley centred, most people expected the centre-forward to go for goal, but Dixie's

Dixie Dean was the undisputed king of Goodison in 1931, scoring four in a crushing 9-2 win over Leicester City. His big dream, however, was to hoist aloft the FA Cup which he did in 1933. This historic picture shows Dean with the trophy on his shoulder, flanked by his delighted teammates. Albert Geldard holds the match-ball.

eye for a better opening saw him calmly nodding the ball back to Johnson who struck the ball so hard, McLaren didn't even see it, let alone save it.

Dean now decided to increase his own tally although he was aided by the 'keeper. He met Stein's centre with a firm header and while McLaren got to the ball, he succeeded only in patting it back into the forward's path and this time Dean steered the ball into the corner of the net.

So the Blues were four goals to the good and looking as if they had twice as many players on the field as their opponents. Leicester finally responded on the break, Hind driving home to pull a goal back shortly before half-time. But Everton would add three more goals in the space of 11 minutes at the start of the second half with the kind of attacking football that had the fans purring.

Johnson sent a header beyond McLaren after 46 minutes following an accurate Stein corner. White made

it 6-1 without knowing too much about it. Gee thumped the ball forward and the 'keeper moved wide of his goal expecting to collect. But the driven forward ball glanced off White and sped into the far corner. Dean secured his hat-trick with a soaring header from a Critchley corner, but Everton were not satisfied with seven.

They even scored an own-goal, Sagar turning a corner-kick under his own bar after 62 minutes. But the rout continued when Dean claimed his fourth and Everton's eighth following a skilful run and centre by Stein. The Blues were simply unstoppable and Clark scored his first top-flight goal with a brilliant long-range effort to make it nine. It was attacking football of the highest quality. Everton were not so much a team as a goal machine.

Everton: Sagar; Williams, Cresswell, Clark, Gee, Thomson, Critchley, White, Dean, Johnson, Stein.
Attendance: 33,513

Tommy White was a first-class partner for the powerful Dixie Dean. Here, White plunders a goal in a 4-2 League victory over Sunderland in January 1932.

The Old One-Two
. . .Champs At The Double

Saturday, 30 April 1932

Everton 1 Bolton Wanderers 0

THE lowest point in Everton's long and distinguished history was undoubtedly season 1929-30 when the Blues finished rock-bottom in the First Division and found themselves relegated for the first time ever, a humbling experience for one of the League's founder members.

Wounded pride proved to be an inspirational weapon and not only did the Blues bounce back at the first time of asking with a convincing Second Division championship success in 1930-31, they followed it up with a storming top-flight title triumph just 12 months later.

There were rousing scenes at Goodison Park as Everton claimed the game's greatest honour for the fourth time in their history with a 1-0 victory over Bolton Wanderers.

Ernest Edwards — writing in the 'Football Echo' under his famous pseudonym 'Bee' — stuck a little blow for all Blues' fans in his colourful report when he said: *Everton have often been chided that there was one record they could never claim compared with Liverpool, their neighbours. They had never won the Second Division championship and the First Division championship in successive years. Evertonians replied: 'We could, but we have never been in the Second Division'!*

'Last season Everton duly felt the bump of relegation. They won that League and have now gone on to win Division One with team work, all-round ability and the study of wise play.

'Bee' also quoted captain Dixie Dean, scorer of the only goal against Bolton, in the somewhat flowery manner that was the style of the day. William Ralph was reported to have said: "The lads are splendid. This is a triumph for players who at one time found everything going against them. Today we have touched the peak and Arsenal have again been

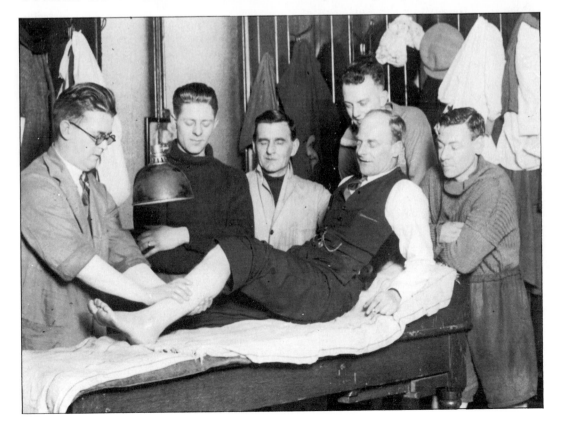

Dean never claimed to be a one-man band. Warney Cresswell, one of the classiest full-backs Everton have ever had, is pictured receiving treatment for a key game in 1932. The attire and the receding hairline gives Warney the look of a businessman rather than a top-class footballer, but he was at the peak of his playing powers and eventually completed 306 appearances for the Blues. Looking on are Sagar, White and Rigby with trainer Harry Cooke (centre).

put to second place. I want to thank all our players for their brilliant work.''

The kind of 'brilliant work' Dean referred to was there for all to see in the Championship clincher against Bolton. The game had an extra edge because the Wanderers side featured cente-half Tom Griffiths, a rangy defender who had played for Everton for four years between 1926 and 1930. Indeed, he had made 26 appearances during that fateful relegation season. Now he was back, ironically trying to prevent his old club from clinching the League Championship.

As skipper of Wanderers, he exchanged a few amusing words with his former captain Dean and as they tossed up the heavens opened and there was a loud clap of thunder. Was someone up there trying to tell Tom something. Dean opted to attack the Gwladys Street End in the first half, taking advantage of a strong northerly wind. The Blues suffered an early blow when Gee had to go off for treatment on a knee injury. He hobbled back into play, bandaged and unlikely to do himself any justice in a strongly contested affair.

Everton had an anxious moment when Sagar raced out without much chance of intercepting the ball. Butler was able to get in a shot with the goalkeeper out of position, but fortunately the ball flew high and wide. Gee went off again, but reappeared with a new bandage and a real determination to play a part. In the meantime, Everton recovered their composure to build up some excellent attacking moves, one ending with the lively Dunn trying to head the ball out of the hands of 'keeper Jones.

But Dean was being well-marshalled by Griffiths and the Blues' play deteriorated as quickly as it had improved. The game had gone dead and so had the crowd until a voice boomed out from the paddock: 'Play Up Everton!'

Johnson responded with a clever overhead kick that rebounded back off the bar. Gee had battled on bravely, but he had to leave the field shortly before

half-time, reducing the Champions-elect to ten men.

Thomson went to centre-half and Johnson to left-half. As often happens in adversity, the weakened team now raised their game to cover for their loss. Dean claimed possession and seemed in no hurry to move the ball on, but it had the Bolton defenders scurrying round to try and cover. The centre-forward finally brought Critchley into play and he cleverly hooked the ball over his head before going for a strong shot which produced a corner.

The kick was punched back out towards the touchline by Jones, but the irrepressible Dunn hoisted it straight back in. Dean, seeing his moment, stretched his neck muscles and sent a solid header towards the furthest post. The tall Jones was unable to keep it out, but then he would not be the first or last to be beaten by Dean's aerial

Everton, League Champions 1931-32. Back row (left to right): Harry Cooke (trainer), Clark, Williams, Sagar, Gee, Cresswell, Britton. Front: Critchley, White, Dean, Johnson, Stein, Thomson.

power. It gave Everton an all-important interval lead and the ten men would defend it with tremendous character after the break.

The brave Gee attempted one more return, at inside-left, but the first time he touched the ball he grimaced with pain and he headed back to the touchline.

A rainstorm now came over the ground as well as a storm of Bolton attacks. Sagar was at his best in this spell and Everton did not stand on ceremony in the closing stages, hammering the ball out at the first sign of danger. By now skipper Dean was drifting deeper and deeper to help out his defence. He desperately wanted to get his hands on that Championship and the referee's whistle finally ensured he would.

The title had been won by clever football, all-round superior team work, leadership and unselfishness, said one report. And Anfield's historic 'double'

had been equalled with Everton's very own version of the old one-two.

Everton: Sagar; Williams, Cresswell, Clark, Gee, Thomson, Critchley, Dunn, Dean, Johnson, Stein.
Attendance: 28,546

There was plenty to shout about at Goodison in the 1930s and they were able to do it from the roof tops, courtesy of this searchlight-type loudspeaker which was installed above the Main Stand. The church is visible beyond the roof. This piece of '30s high-tech gadgetry was said to be able to carry sound a distance of two miles and was used for musical broadcasts and general announcements.

Goodison's Greatest Ever Cup Tie?

Wednesday, 30 January 1935

Everton 6 Sunderland 4

ASK Evertonians to name the greatest ever FA Cup tie seen on Goodison Park and modern enthusiasts will inevitably go for the sensational 4-4 draw in 1991, a clash of titanic proportions between Everton and Liverpool.

But senior fans will immediately recall a replay battle that unfolded in 1935 and which took the breath away of the 59,213 supporters who were fortunate enough to be present on a memorable Wednesday afternoon. One fan suggested that everybody should have been charged on the way out, as well as the way in, so entertaining was this fifth-round affair.

The crowd revelled in ten goals, six of them hitting the back of the Sunderland net. The Blues were never in arrears, twice Sunderland drew level and every goal was scored with a shot. It left the 'Echo's' Ernest Edwards posing this question: *Has there ever been a greater game of skill in the mud in any League or Cup match? We all keep our memory cells filled with noteworthy sporting occasions, but this latest 6-4 game will top the lot by reason of its two goals in the two closing minutes, by the ordering off of a manger of the visiting side, and by the multitudinous moments of dramatic skill and art.*

The referee, Mr Pinckston of Aston Villa, was saluted for the way he made the players get on with the game. Sunderland swept up the field with adroit passes and combination, only to be mediocre near the goalmouth — they scored only four!

Everton won because they had that extra bit of finishing power. Jackie Coulter's three, Albert Geldard's two and Alex Stevenson's solo effort stood out boldly. Jimmy Cunliffe, that outstanding inside-forward, played for much of the later stages in a state of semi-consciousness, having been badly concussed.

The ground was so packed that the crowd broke on to the line in the early stages without serious consequences. But many people had to be lifted out by the police and the ambulancemen, particularly in the Goodison Road

enclosure. The fans were finally able to concentrate on the action and Coulter cheered everybody with an opener after 14 minutes. It was not a great strike, but rather a tribute to Stevenson's early work. The fact that the Blues were in front was reason enough to celebrate.

Coulter made it 2-0 after 31 minutes, the Irishman moving in to crash a Geldard centre into the net. But Sunderland were far from beaten and David reduced the arrears four minutes before the interval. There were still many people outside the ground and there was a report that a considerable number had tried to rush the gates.

When the second half got underway, Roker star goalkeeper Thorpe was warned by the referee for swinging on the bar like a trapeze artiste.

The diminutive Stevenson now thrilled the crowd. The smallest man on the field tried to charge Thorpe over the goal-line, much to the amusement

> **Factfile:** Everton, having won this Cup classic, now beat Derby County 3-1 at Goodison with Coulter the goal hero again. He scored two and Dean grabbed the other. But in the sixth round, also at home, Bolton Wanderers shocked the Merseysiders 2-1, even though Coulter was on the mark again.

of the fans. Stevenson appeared to have settled it 15 minutes from time with a close-range effort after Dean had headed in.

But Connor had the home fans edgy with a fine effort to make it 3-2 and Gurney equalised with possibly the last kick of the 90 minutes. He was probably the only man in the ground not to see his overhead kick go in. It was now 3-3 and extra-time was called into play.

Before the match resumed, Sunderland manager John Cockrane was ordered off the field as he tried to coach his players. Coulter claimed his treble two minutes into the extra spell, but the yo-yo nature of the game continued when Connor made it 4-4.

With a second replay now looking a certainty, Geldard took matters into his own hands and he put the Blues in front with an outstretched boot from a Dean header. In the closing stages, he finished off the visitors when he hoisted the ball high into the area and it sailed in over the heads of Dean and defender Thorpe.

Everton: Sagar; Cook, Jones, Britton, Gee, Thomson, Geldard, Cunliffe, Dean, Stevenson and Coulter.

Attendance: 59,213

Everton and Tranmere Rovers were involved in some transfer business on 13 March 1936. The Blues captured famous Prenton striker Bunny Bell who, on Boxing Day 1935, had set a League record by scoring nine for Rovers against Oldham Athletic (he also missed a penalty!) Bell (right) is seen putting pen to paper for Theo Kelly, while Everton's Archie Clarke signs for Mr R.T.Knowles, the Tranmere secretary. Incredibly, Bell failed to make an impact at Goodison and managed only 14 appearances (although he did score nine goals) before returning to continue his scoring exploits with Rovers.

The Master And The Pupil

Wednesday, 3 March 1937

Everton 7 Leeds United 1

THIS was a significant day for Evertonians. It was the game in which they saw the master and the pupil in action together for the very first time on home soil. The Blues had paid Burnley £6,500 for the services of teenage sensation Tommy Lawton, a Bolton lad who had scored a remarkable 570 goals in three seasons of schoolboy football.

Lawton had netted on his Everton debut at Wolves, but had very little to celebrate. The Merseysiders lost 7-2, lacking the experience and attacking know-how of Dixie Dean. The great man returned to partner Lawton in the subsequent away game at Birmingham, but once again Everton tasted defeat, going down 2-0.

Now they entertained Leeds United at Goodison Park, a game that captured the interest of fans on both sides of Stanley Park. Obviously the chance to see Dean and Lawton in tandem was of particular interest to the Goodison faithful. At the same time, here was a match that could help ease Liverpool's relegation worries. For once, Reds' fans desperately wanted the old enemy to win.

But there was a strange twist. Making his debut up front for Leeds was former Anfield favourite, South African-born Gordon Hodgson. It meant the day had genuine possiblities.

The previous weekend, Merseyside had suffered blizzard conditions. The Goodison pitch was heavy to say the least. At the toss-up, Dean flipped the coin on to the back of his hand, rather than let it drop to the floor in customary

On 3 March 1937, Dean and Lawton played at home together for the first time. The match was a seven-goal sensation. Here three of Goodison most loved centre-forwards meet at dinner in the 1960s. From left to right: Lawton, Alex Young and Dean.

A portrait of Cliff Britton who, with Joe Mercer and Stan Cullis, formed one of the finest half-back lines England have ever had. Britton was a great 1930s favourite.

famous partner. He siezed control from a corner, hesitated momentarily while he selected his spot and unleashed a solid effort into the bottom left-hand corner. It was looking good for Everton — and Liverpool!

The fans were fascinated by the new attacking partnership, although it was noted that no one outshone Dean for endeavour in the heavy conditions. His heading was also of the highest class, but then this aspect of his game rarely dropped below outstanding.

Lawton had been making a name for himself with his speed of thought. He would collect the ball and deliver a shot so quickly that opponents were constantly caught out.

But this was a day for shared honours. All five Everton forwards managed to get on the scoresheet, Dean adding to his tally in the second half, aided and abetted by Stevenson (two), Geldard and Gillick.

Leeds scored a single consolation goal, swamped in the Goodison mud.

Lawton had made himself an instant favourite. He would go on to claim Dean's famous number nine jersey and score 70 goals in 95 games for the Blues before the war interrupted his Goodison career. He was transferred to Chelsea for £11,500, Everton making a 100 per cent profit on what they had paid for him. Notts County later paid a record £20,000 for the centre-forward's services and after spells with Brentford and Arsenal, his career record was 231 goals in 390 League games.

The Goodison crowd never forgot Tommy. Everton staged a testimonial game for him in 1972, a full 27 years after his last wartime appearance for the Blues. Fittingly, a Great Britain XI provided the opposition and the occasion raised £6,500. As he walked on to the pitch to take a special bow, his mind no doubt drifted back to that Goodison debut game of 1937 and the seven goals that flew into the Leeds United net. Happy days indeed.

Everton: Sagar; Jackson, Cook, Britton, Gee, Mercer, Geldard, Lawton, Dean, Stevenson, Gillick.

Attendance: 17,064

fashion because the pitch was so muddy.

But it was a bright afternoon and the stands were packed with a large gathering of scouts and managers from rival clubs. Everton attacked the Stanley Park End in the first half. Hodgson was determined to impress on a Merseyside stage and he went close with one of his famous headers from a dangerous corner.

Dean showed his strength by charging Holley to the ground and he powered on through the mud to go extremely close. Lawton now came to prominence with a pacy run and a first-class shot which McInroy took with both hands. The conditions did not seem to suit the visiting defenders. The mud was six inches deep around their goal, but the home forwards seemed to revel in it, showing excellent control.

Geldard's body swerve was the starting point for many Everton attacks. Dean was inevitably the man on the end of these moves and he rifled home a shot from a central position 25 yards out that flew into the corner of the net to make it 1-0.

Lawton was not to be outdone by his

Dixie's Heading Out!

Saturday, 11 December 1937

Everton 1 Birmingham 1

THE incomparable William Ralph 'Dixie' Dean scored an astonishing 377 goals for Everton in 431 appearances. He was a legend in his own lifetime — a man whose 60 League goals in the 1927-28 season will never be beaten.

His greatest moments in the game have been well documented — his scoring feats for England, his record-breaking triumph against Arsenal and his inspirational role in the 1933 FA Cup Final against Manchester City.

But what was it like at Goodison Park the day the greatest centre-forward the world has ever seen played his last game for the Blues? What we tend to forget is that it was just another game for the fans. They didn't know the great man was wearing his famous number nine jersey for the last time.

If they had, there is every good chance it would have been a gala occasion with the famous stadium bursting at the seams, just as it was on 7 May 1928 when Dean brought the house down with the hat-trick against Arsenal that would make him immortal.

Hundreds of games and hundreds of goals on, he was selected for only his fifth League outing of the season on a bitterly cold December day in 1937 with Tommy Lawton out injured. Incredibly, the match was in doubt until 2pm with the surface covered in a skin of ice. The referee inspected the pitch at 12.30pm and, according to the 'Football Echo', found it was hard as flint.

A second check an hour later suggested that the ground was softening and the official declared he would give it another half-hour, at which point the gates were thrown open. The heavily sanded surface still seemed fairly treacherous but the 'Echo' would later report: *All 22 men gave an excellent display considering the icy conditions.*

Before the kick-off Dean got a fine reception from the small crowd of just over 17,000. Once a hero, always a hero. He responded in the first minute with a neat header to Cunliffe, who should have done better from an excellent position.

Then Birmingham — they did not add 'City' to their title until 1945 — moved forward almost immediately to claim a shock lead. Richards made a pass along the touchline which Morris collected and he wasted no time in hammering in a shot. Goalkeeper Morton pulled the ball from under his crossbar but he fumbled it. He tried to recover, but the ball had crossed the line and Everton were down.

Football remained a tricky business on the rock-hard pitch and it was possible to hear the ice cracking under the players' feet. Dean, Stevenson and Cunliffe conjured up an outstanding passing move that was described as favouring a cricket pitch rather than an ice-bound football ground.

Dixie was playing in a slightly withdrawn role behind his fellow forwards. Every time the Everton 'keeper launched the ball forward, he was winning it with his head and directing headers to Stevenson and Cunliffe. Dean might have been in the twilight of his career but he was still the undisputed king of the air.

The pitch now caught out 'keeper Morton, enjoying a run in the continued absence of another Goodison legend, Ted Sagar. Morton tried to race across his own goalmouth as Beattie threatened, but he fell headlong and the crowd gasped as the shot flew narrowly wide.

As usual, though, the fans looked to Dean to find a way through. He produced a fiery drive which brought a roar from the crowd as it flew wide and it proved an inspirational moment because Everton levelled matters with their next attack. Geldard was the scorer with a long-range effort that was reported to have left his foot *like a stone from a catapult*.

It was his first League goal for nine months and Dean's broad smile as he

Dixie Dean welcomes new winger Torry Gillick to Goodison in December 1935, an £8,000 buy from Glasgow Rangers. Gillick would be a provider for Dean and score many goals himself. He figured in Dean's final Goodison match against Birmingham in 1937.

patted his teammate on the back summed up the mood.

The final whistle now loomed. As Dean trudged off he would not have realised that he had pulled on a royal blue shirt at Goooodison for the very last time. It was the end of a goalscoring era, the like of which we will never see again. **Everton:** Morton, Cook, J.Jones, Britton, T.G.Jones, Mercer, Geldard, Cunliffe, Dean, Stevenson, Gillick. *Attendance: 17,018*

Factfile: Dean subsequently played in a friendly at Halifax on 12 February 1938. His last game was the Liverpool Senior Cup semi-final at South Liverpool on 9 March 1938. He scored the last of Everton's four winning goals and two days later joined Notts County.

An example of how Dixie Dean's name was exploited in a commerical sense. A famous coat company wanted the Everton star to model a 'gangster' style mac and hat. He insisted they use the entire team, hence this remarkable picture with the great man holding the FA Cup for good measure. The full line-up is: Back row (left to right): Billy Cook, Ted Sagar, Jock Thomson, Dean, Cliff Britton, Jimmy Stein, Tommy Johnson, Warney Cressell. Front: Harry Cooke (trainer), Tommy White, Jimmy Dunn, Albert Geldard.

Dixie Has His 60 Goals — Gordon His 60 Years!

DIXIE Dean scored his 60 goals to become a legendary figure. One of his contemporaries can now claim a very special '60' all of his own, but in Gordon Watson's case, it's 60 years of service to the club he joined from Blyth Spartans in January 1933.

If you want to know about the old days, Goodison Park as it was in that famous pre-war era when Dean, Lawton, Mercer, Sagar and the rest were the men of the people, you go and talk to Gordon. You will find him conducting one of the many 'tours' around Goodison or even working on the door of one of the executive lounges. He has been a truly wonderful servant to the Blues, first as a player who mixed tight control with fierce tackling, and later as trainer, promotions man and now official guide. The North-East accent is still in evidence, but here is a man steeped in Merseyside tradition.

He paints a wonderful picture of the players of the 1930s, the men who wore tough leather boots up to their ankles with solid toe-caps, kicked a 'casey' that seemed to weigh a ton when wet, lived alongside the fans and mixed freely with them, both before and after matches, and earned next to nothing for their labours on the field, even though they were often playing to crowds that dwarf the modern average attendance.

Gordon said: "Most of the players lived near to the ground, many of them in Goodison Avenue behind the Stanley Park End. It meant that the likes of Dean, Dunn, Stein and even old trainer Harry Cooke would walk to the game with the fans.

"I lived in Harewood Street, just off Breck Road and then in Ince Avenue. Me and Torry Gillick used to walk through Anfield Cemetery to get to Goodison on match days. There would be hundreds of fans walking with us. If you got beat, you stayed in the dressing-room for two hours after the match, frightened to go out and face the walk home.

"If Liverpool beat us, we would go home and then refuse to go out for three days!

Harry Cooke – Everton's dedicated trainer and the original magic sponge man. Dean once said: "Without him, I would never have broken that record."

"Goodison Park was very different to the stadium we see today. For instance, there was no stand at the Gwladys Street End when I first arrived in 1933. It was all concrete steps with an old scoreboard at the back to display the half-time scores. If the weather was bad, it was possible to do sprints under the steps behind the Gwladys Street End.

"There was a little gymnasium where the main car-park is now. We would get old balls, take the bladder out and stuff them with paper like medicine balls. We used to practise throwing them against the wall on the Bullens Road side. Dixie used to see how far and how high he could throw them. We would play wall tennis and we also did a lot of roadwork.

"When we first reported back to training, the first four days involved long road runs from Goodison. We would run down as far as the Jolly Miller pub on Queen's Drive, turn down towards West Derby Village, reach the Crown Pub at the top of Walton Hall Avenue via Long Lane and then make our way back down to the ground.

"The old club car-park was originally grassed. The 'A' and 'B' teams used to play there. It was also a centre for the training. In those days, there was no collective work as such. You would just come in, get stripped and go out on the field. The trainer would tell you what to do and you just got on with it. No one would shirk the work, even though we never trained as a group and never really got the ball out."

Gordon revealed that the only time

Will Cuff, one of Goodison's greatest servants, had his hands on both the FA Cup and League Championship trophy in Everton's balmy days between the wars, but not in the same years.

the players saw a ball during the week was on Tuesday mornings when there was shooting practice. Those Tuesday sessions involved the full-backs going behind the goals to field and return the balls. They had big playing staffs in those days and 30 to 40 pros would be out there. If you came in early, you got more shots with three or four goals set up. Now and again, a few crosses would be played in, but mainly it was shooting.

There were never any complicated team discussions concerning moves and tactics. Gordon said: "You simply learned by the experience of the older players. If you played in an away match, you would arrange to 'room' with a partner who could pass on bits of help and information. I would go with Billy Cook or Jock Thompson. These were players who worked little things out themselves for corner-kicks and the like.

"But there was never any organised coaching. You simply learned by your mistakes. The other players would make sure you didn't make the same mistake twice. There were no tactical meetings before matches. Before the season, they would call us all together and say: 'Look, this is Everton Football Club. Whether you are travelling home or away, we want you properly dressed with a collar and tie.' This was probably the only time we were addressed collectively. But we still had a tremendous side with some wonderful players."

Gordon often found himself 12th man. The sheer size of the squad and the quality of the team meant that competition was intense. The lad from the North-East was an excellent all-rounder and he would play in every outfield position except centre-forward. Gordon would play a part in the 1938-39 Championship success before the war interrupted his career.

In his early days, Dixie Dean was the undisputed star turn and yet there was never any petty jealousy amongst his contemporaries, helped by the fact that players were paid exactly the same, regardless of their pedigree. Dean was very level-headed and never sought any special privileges.

Gordon recalls: "When the club got to the Cup Final in 1933, I had only just come down from the North-East. There was a 50 shilling tailor on Walton Road. They came up to the ground and asked Dixie to advertise one of their suits. There was an ice-cream parlour next door called Fusco's and they wanted to get in on the act, picturing Dixie licking one of their ice creams.

"He refused to do it unless the whole team was involved. There is a famous photograph knocking round of the lads in a line, all wearing long raincoats down to their ankles and trilby hats. Dixie could have taken it on himself and made a few bob, but he wanted the squad to benefit from the Cup success.

"It was a big gesture because the players were only earning £8 a week and even this used to go down to £6 in the close season. When I finished as a player in 1949, I was on £20 a week with £2 for a win bonus. That was the most I ever earned as a player.

"I can remember when we won the Championship in 1939, secretary Theo Kelly took us all out for the day to Blackpool. He gave me and the wife 2s

6d (12½p) and said, 'Go out and enjoy yourself.' We thought it was great."

Gordon never used to drink, but it was a favourite pastime for many of the big stars. There was nothing unusual about a player having a drink on a Friday night in those days, regardless of the game the next day. The legendary Dixie was quite a lad.

Gordon recalls a famous story about the greatest striker that has ever lived. He said: "Chelsea had signed a centre-half called Peter O'Dowd. I think they paid £7,000 for him. He wrote in the 'Echo' and the 'Evening Express' that Dixie wouldn't get a kick in the game at Goodison on the Saturday.

"The night before the game, Dixie went out and got a little bit worse for wear. The trainer kept him at Goodison all night. They slept in the trainer's room by the old dressing-rooms, lying on the skips and the St John's Ambulance rugs. The trainer went home and brought back a flask of hot coffee, no doubt thinking that O'Dowd would be able to live by his word and play Dean off the park. Dixie went out the next day and scored five! Everton won the match 7-2."

The players were always up to different tricks. Little Alex Stevenson, one of the finest ball-players of his era, and his right-wing partner Wally Boyes, were both known as 'Mickey Mouse' because of the pranks they used to get up to.

Gordon said: "You would get back to your room on an away trip and find your bedclothes gone. Even the directors were not immune from the tricksters. Dean was another who was always game for a laugh. I remember an occasion on a bridge above Chesterfield Station. He kept shouting down to a policeman just for fun: 'Aye, Aye Copper!'

"The next minute the constable was up on the platform asking who had been doing all the shouting. He took Dixie into this room and we all thought he was going to arrest him because it was all so serious. Suddenly they came out, side by side and smoking cigars. That was typical Dixie."

Dean was a giant figure, on and off the field. When he was playing, he never used to like to have his shirt tucked right down inside his shorts, but at the same time, the players were not allowed to have them hanging out, George Best fashion. Gordon recalls that Dixie used to get the trainer to cut his shirt level with his shorts so when he jumped you could often see his back. Whether it was because he felt freer that way or felt it helped to keep him cool is open to debate. He was just a character and a half.

The players didn't just have to cope with poor pitches and ankle-deep mud in Watson's day, they also had to play with a ball that became very heavy when it was wet.

Gordon said: "I think the regulation weight was 28 ounces, but it soaked up the water and would often split your forehead if you headed the lace. Of course, they used to say that Cliff Britton was so talented, he would centre the ball so the lace faced away from Dixie.

"And when the goals went in, which was often, there were no mass celebrations or players jumping up on to hoardings to punch the air. The scorer would just turn and jog back into position. There would be the odd shout of 'well done' but that was it. Finding the net was all part and parcel of the day to day business."

So was looking after each other. Gordon remembers a game at Brentford. He said: "I was only reserve, but Warney Cresswell took ill. They told me two hours before the match that I was playing and I was a bag of nerves in the dressing-room. As we were going out, Dixie said, 'Get next to me,' and so I followed him up the tunnel.

"They had a player called Davis and I remember he hit me early in the game, knocking me down and winding me. Jock Thomson just ran past and said, 'Leave it to me'. A few minutes later, Davis was lying down and holding his mouth. Jock was there, helping to pick him up. The lad didn't know what, or who, hit him. That's the way it was. There was an incredible spirit and we looked out for each other."

The rewards were not high considering the attendances, but Gordon still revels in the stories and never misses a chance to pass on the many legendary tales as he conducts his Goodison tours at the age of 80, the definitive Everton expert.

Members of Everton's 1938-39 Championship squad are pictured at Lime Street Station. Left to right: Boyes, T.G.Jones, Cook, Caskie, Stevenson, Lawton, Gillick, Sagar, Watson, Mercer, Greenhalgh.

Champions —
And Then It's War

Saturday, 29 April 1939

Everton 3 Aston Villa 0

EVERTON finished the 1930s as they had begun it, their name on everybody's lips.

Herbert Chapman's legendary Arsenal held sway in the middle of the decade, but the Blues finished the 1938-39 season back on top of the pack.

They would effectively be 'Champions' for seven years with regional football the name of the game during the war years.

It was the season that Everton clinched the title on the day they lost! They went down 2-1 at Charlton, their first defeat in seven games, but Wolverhampton Wanderers failure to win at Bolton meant the Merseysiders could not be caught in the remaining two games.

The final home League game was against Aston Villa and the newly-installed Champs desperately wanted to turn it on for the fans. Manager-secretary Theo Kelly had built a new team around exciting young players like Joe Mercer, a wing-half with a superb tactical brain and Tommy Lawton, who filled Dixie Dean's striking boots so superbly that many claimed he was an even better centre-forward than the maestro.

This in itself is a subject that could be debated around the clock. Lawton was generous to say that there was no one better than Dixie. Perhaps the argument should end there.

But there is no disputing the fact that Lawton was a very special player, possessing two outstanding feet and being virtually unbeatable in the air. He led the line in that final home game against Villa, having already plundered 34 League goals in 36 games.

The crowd was not as big as many thought it would be but the new Champions were still showered with confetti and given a great ovation when they emerged from the tunnel.

The football was not as good as it might have been in the opening exchanges but the ball was lively and a strong wind did not help the players.

Everton soon settled down. Defender Allen showed his fear of Lawton when he hurriedly kicked into touch rather than taking any risks but this safety clearance led to the opening goal after 11 minutes. The scorer was Bentham, a man whose strikes were few and far between. Nevertheless, it was an excellent effort, a powerhouse shot that goalkeeper Rutherford never even saw.

Gillick provided the knockout punch when he made it 2-0 after 23 minutes, but in doing so he took one on the chin and was carried off unconscious. The stockily-built winger, having made a goalwards header from Caskie's free-kick, was instantaneously caught full in the face as Rutherford tried to punch clear. He did not see the ball hit the

back of the net and was lifted to the touchline where he received lengthy treatment before he was able to continue, holding a handkerchief to a bloody nose.

The Blues now had the opportunity to further increase their lead when Villa conceded a penalty after a Bentham header was handled by Iverson on the line. Cook was Everton's spot-kick expert and he scored with his usual confidence to make it 3-0 with just 29 minutes gone.

Surprisingly, Lawton had not figured in the scoring. It was not to be his day — three cannonball drives rebounding clear off defenders. The Blues strolled through the second half and while there were no further goals, the crowd saluted the Champions warmly on the final whistle.

No one enjoying the carnival atmosphere at Goodison that day realised what was just around the corner. It

Scottish winger Torry Gillick was never far from the action during the 1938-39 Championship success. He is pictured here going close in a 2-0 home win over Brentford. Tommy Lawton (left) grabbed both goals.

Everton met Manchester United in November 1940, in a wartime League North game. This programme cover shows some famous names. Tommy Lawton scored four and Alex Stevenson also netted in a 5-2 victory. Johnny Carey, the United number ten, later became Everton's manager.

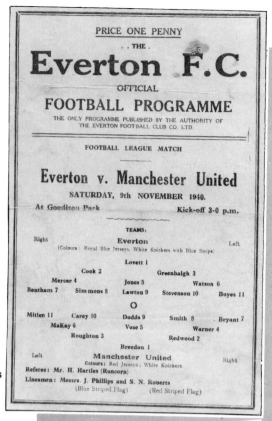

Off to war in 1939 and the 'Echo's' George Green warns the enemy about some Merseyside sporting heroes, including Everton's Tommy Lawton.

Goodison Park was hit by German bombs in September 1940. The club received £5,000 from the War Damage Commission to carry out essential repair work.

would soon be war games only for the likes of Sergeant-Major Mercer as Adolf Hitler drew the world into a bitter conflict that would last six long years. **Everton:** Sagar; Cook, Greenhalgh, Mercer, T.G.Jones, Watson, Gillick, Bentham, Lawton, Stevenson, Caskie. *Attendance: 23,667*

The Blues 1938-39
Football League
Championship side.
Back row (left to
right): Lawton,
T.G.Jones, Sagar,
H.Cooke (trainer),
Mercer, Greenhalgh.
Front: W.Cook,
Gillick, Bentham,
Thomson,
Stevenson, Boyes.
The young mascot is
one J.Shannon.

The Everton squad in 1948-49. Back row (left to right): Juliussen, Falder, Catterick, Hedley, Lewis, Fielding, Eglington, Saunders, Farrell, Humphreys, Greenhalgh. Middle: T.G.Jones, Corr, Dugdale, Pinchbeck, Powell, Burnett, Sagar, Cameron, Higgins, Cookson, Clinton, Lindley, H Cooke (trainer). Front: Boyes, Watson, Stevenson, Bentham, McCormick, Lello, Wainwright, Grant.

Bring In The Crowds — 78,299 Of Them!

Saturday, 18 September 1948

Everton 1 Liverpool 1

IN the soccer-mad post-war years, crowds of 50,000 plus were not so much unusual as the order of the day. When Liverpool crossed the park in season 1947-48 to stage an FA Cup tie against Manchester United, a staggering 74,721 people passed through the Goodison turnstiles to set a new attendance record for the ground. United had to make the venue switch because of war damage to Old Trafford.

Few people thought the attendance would be surpassed. Yet when Liverpool returned early in the following campaign to face the old enemy in a League game, it was clear that an historic day was on the cards.

The famous old stadium was bursting at the seams and the gates were finally locked with 78,299 fans inside the ground. It remains the record attendance and will never be beaten, successive ground safety rules reducing the Goodison capacity almost by half.

The 'Football Echo' reported that there were many casualities, not least because of the swaying in the paddock. The teams came out side by side and the roar of anticipation inside was matched only by the roar of frustration outside where thousands were locked out!

Stevenson was Everton's captain and he won the toss, opting to attack the Gwladys Street goal in the first half. Modern tradition dictates that the Blues defend that end before the break, but this was clearly not the case on this memorable afternoon.

Liverpool's best chance in the opening exchanges fell to Liddell, but Sagar claimed his splendid teasing centre under the bar. Liddell then tried one of those pile-driver shots for which he was famous. The ball rebounded out to

Balmer who lifted his shot over the top.

The Reds were on top, but Sidlow had to concede a corner after Stevenson cracked in a shot from the left. The visitors were soon encouraging their vast army of fans with a series of determined attacks but T.G. Jones was immaculate in the heart of the home defence. Cool and controlled, he extricated himself from any difficult situation with a classical touch to a better-placed teammate.

At the same time, Stevenson was delivering some outstanding passes, linking well with Boyes to cause the Liverpool defence a certain amount of anxiety. Boyes beat his man and centred across goal for Fielding to head back into the middle.

Boyes, the instigator of the move, had followed up and Sidlow was forced to make a useful save. At this stage, Everton were playing some outstanding football.

Liddell was not having the best of games against Bentham and Saunders.

But the Anfield star could never be ignored and a powerful run and shot forced Sagar to concede a corner on the stroke of half-time.

The Reds came out fighting after the interval, determined to make the all-important breakthrough and Sagar had to be on his guard to deny both Fagan and Shannon.

Stevenson, a player who could turn on a sixpence, raised the home spirits with a feint that bamboozled two defenders, but the Blues were unable to cash in on his skill.

Sagar made an absolutely stunning save after Fagan had volleyed goalwards in spectacular fashion. The ball was powering towards the corner of the net when the 'keeper plunged down to turn it away. Late in the half, Jones had to leave the field for treatment to a leg injury. He was off for only a matter of minutes, but Liverpool cashed in to score.

Payne made a good run and flicked

Theo Kelly, acknowledged as Everton's first-ever manager (1939-48). Earlier, coaches, directors and committees had been responsible for team selection.

the ball wide to Shannon in the outside-right berth. His outstanding cross invited Liddell to crash a shot goalwards. It failed to reach the target, but Fagan was on the spot to cash in with a solid and accurate shot into the far corner.

Liverpool's delight was shortlived. A Boyes corner caused panic in the visitors' defence. The ball was finally returned to Boyes, whose rocket shot beat Sidlow all ends up, only to be tipped over the bar by defender Shepherd.

Dodds took the resulting penalty and whilst Sidlow got his hands to the ball, he could not keep it out of the net. There were only six minutes left in which neither side managed to conjure up a winner. But it had been an historic day on the terraces. Like Dean's 60 goals, here was an attendance that would stand the test of time.

Left: A fine action picture of centre-forward Jock Dodds in 1948. Real name Ephraim Dodds, 'Jock' was a giant no-nonsense striker who had previously been with Huddersfield, Sheffield United and Blackpool. He scored 37 goals in 58 Everton appearances.

Right: A portrait of outstanding inside-forward Alex Stevenson, who scored 90 goals in 271 appearances between 1933-34 and 1948-49.

Below: While the players put opponents through the mangle out on the pitch, Miss Buchanan put the kit through the electric mangle in the Goodison laundry, watched here by 'A' team trainer George Thompson. This picture was taken in 1949.

Everton: Sagar; Saunders, Hedley, Bentham, T.G. Jones, Watson, Powell, Fielding, Dodds, Stevenson, Boyes. *Attendance: 78,299 (some reports initially gave the figure as 78,599)*

Factfile: On the Monday immediately following this record-breaking game it was reported that former Goodison star Cliff Britton would be taking over as manager of the Blues. Britton had been one of the greatest Goodison wing-halves of all time, figuring in the 1933 FA Cup-winning team. Described as a 'student of football', he managed Burnley and enjoyed many triumphs at Turf Moor, inspiring promotion from the Second Division as well as taking the Clarets to Wembley in the FA Cup. He would lead Everton between 1948 and 1956, but major honours eluded him. The Blues went down and were promoted during this spell and had some great runs in the Cup. He finally handed over the reins to Ian Buchan.

England's First Home Defeat Against Foreign Rivals

Wednesday, 21 September 1949

England 0 Republic of Ireland 2

GOODISON Park has the dubious distinction of being the venue when England lost on home soil for the first time to a 'foreign' country — that is to say other than Home International rivals.

The Republic of Ireland were the opposition on a night when the likes of Wilf Mannion, Tom Finney, Billy Wright and the rest found themselves with red faces at the royal blue stadium.

But there was nevertheless an Everton silver lining. The Goodison club's skipper Peter Farrell scored the Republic's second goal five minutes from time, after Con Martin had given them the lead from the penalty spot in the 35th minute.

Another Everton player to enjoy the night was winger Pat Corr, who would be released to non-League Bangor a few weeks later. The Blues would have had a third representative in the Irish side, had Tommy Eglington not been injured.

The 'Liverpool Echo's' report indicates the nation's frustration with England's performance. It said: *To think that Eire, who had extreme difficulty in raising eleven men of sufficient calibre for such a match, should be the first 'outside' country to beat us on home ground. It shows plainly how far we have fallen from the all-conquering England of a few seasons ago. They have fairly put the cat amongst the England selectors' pigeons.*

Finney was the star of the English front line, although his marker, Johnny Carey, later to manage Everton, was described as having a 'brilliant game'. But overall, the home attack was said to have fiddled and finessed to the point of extreme exasperation in the penalty area.

It was a proud night for the Irish, though, particularly the Shamrock Rovers goalkeeper, 22-year-old Tommy Godwin, who was snapped up by Leicester City two weeks later and went on to make over 400 appearances in the Football League.

England: Williams; Mozley, Aston, Wright, Franklin, Dickinson, Harris, Morris, Pye, Mannion, Finney.
Republic of Ireland: Godwin; Carey, A.Herne, W.Walsh, Martin, Moroney, Corr, Farrell, D.Walsh, Desmond, O'Connor.
Attendance: 52,000

It was all smiles at the start of the 1950-51 season as the squad poses before the first game. Little did they know that relegation was on the horizon. Back (left to right): Falder, Saunders, Burnett, Moore, Farrell, Lello. Front: Buckle, Wainwright, Catterick, Eglington, Fielding, Grant.

Despite the heavy snow at the beginning of January 1951, the Blues kept in shape with spring sessions at Goodison. Here, international outside-left Tommy Eglington shows this as the team prepares for a Cup clash at Hull, which was lost 2-0.

Opposite page: The derby game in September 1950 proved a 3-1 losing experience for the Blues. Liverpool skipper Phil Taylor (left) and Everton's Peter Farrell lead out the teams.

The 1950-51 season began brightly enough with a 3-2 home win over Huddersfield Town. The man emerging from the Goodison players' tunnel in the centre of this picture is none other than Harry Catterick, later to become a League and Cup-winning Everton manager.

Heavy snow and plunging temperatures caused problems going into 1951. Everton were 16th in the table and hoping to move away from the danger zone, but they crashed 3-0 at home to Stoke. Moore heads away in this picture, watched by Sagar and Jones, but it proved to be a disappointing afternoon.

That Sinking Feeling

Saturday, 21 April 1951

Everton 1 Aston Villa 2

EVERTON'S final home League game of the season in 1950-51 had disaster written all over it. Only three points had been gained from the previous eight matches and the Blues were staring relegation in the face for only the second time in their long and distinguished history.

The Midlanders were themselves in the danger zone along with Chelsea and

A 2-1 home defeat against Aston Villa in April 1951, proved disastrous for the Blues. It was their last Goodison game before relegation. Peter Farrell was Everton's best player on the day and he sprints in here to try and dispossess Villa forward Thompson.

Sheffield Wednesday. But their plight was of no consequence to the 45,000 Evertonians who turned up at Goodison Park, hoping to play their part in a footballing 'Houdini act'. Could the Blues pull themselves together and snatch crucial points with a view to going into their final two away games with a fighting chance?

Hope springs eternal on the football field, but Everton gave themselves a mountain to climb when they conceded a goal in the very first minute. Villa won the toss and defended the Park End goal which meant their opponents were forced to kick into the sun in the opening period. The start was absolutely sensational.

Villa won a throw-in on the left at the end of their very first attack. Goffin took it and the ball floated over the Everton heads and landed at the feet of Walsh, who quickly invited Dixon to close in on goal from an acute angle. It seemed as if it was too tight a situation

to get in a shot with the vastly experienced Sagar covering the near post, but the forward somehow drilled the ball across the 'keeper and into the far corner of the net.

The Blues were not just playing into the sun, but also into the face of a strong wind. Jones blocked a goal-bound shot from Dorsett. But the home side recovered from these faltering early moments to equalise after just five minutes. Hold picked up a half clearance and whipped the ball across the face of goal. A Villa defender lashed the ball against centre-forward McIntosh and he seized the rebound to make a goal of it.

It was a dire game, reflecting the tension felt by both sides. The crowd groaned to a man when Buckle volleyed an Eglington corner well wide. The game was balanced on a knife-edge at the interval. And so was Everton's First Division status.

As the second half unfolded, Buckle and Aldis clashed heads in a painful

collision. Trainer Cooke advised Buckle to leave the field, but with a sponge held to his damaged cheek, the Everton player sprinted around the goal at the Stanley Park End, determined to carry on. It summed up just how important the result was to the home side.

Ironically, Buckle had only just returned to the field when Villa went in front. It was a disastrous moment for the Blues. Dorsett's centre was flicked on by Dixon and Smith netted from the outside-right position. The crowd's obvious frustration bubbled to the surface.

The Second Division beckoned and respected 'Liverpool Echo' scribe 'Ranger' (Bob Prole) pulled no punches in his Monday column.

He said: *Whether it was just plain jitters or something worse I wouldn't know, but certainly there wasn't enough tenacity or courage on Saturday to send the spectators away with even the slight consolation that the Blues had gone down fighting. Farrell set a great example and Potts ran himself almost to a standstill, but most of the rest seemed as infirm of purpose and lacking in determination as though it made no difference whether they won or lost.*

Goodison had certainly seen better days. The Merseysiders were going down.

Everton: Sagar; Moore, Rankin, Grant, T.E.Jones, Farrell, Buckle, Hold, McIntosh, Potts, Eglington.
Attendance: 45,254

Peter Farrell makes a flying clearance ahead of Villa's Thompson on 21 April 1951, but Everton are heading into the Second Division.

Eddie Wainwright, Peter Farrell and Tommy Eglington take to the air in training in February 1952.

Opposite page, top: Harry Potts playing head tennis under the Gwladys Street Stand in 1951. This was common practice when the weather was bad. Potts later earned fame as manager of Burnley.

Opposite page, bottom: Former Everton players, on the staff in the early 1950s, are pictured here 'putting the boot in' – but only for repairs. Messrs Watson, Bentham, Leyfield and Borthwick at work in the Goodison 'cobbler's shop'.

113

Can you recognise yourself in this fans' group, taken en-route to Villa Park in the Cup in February 1953.

Blood And Thunder Cup Triumph

Saturday, 14 February 1953

Everton 2 Manchester United 1

THOSE who were lucky enough to be at Goodison Park for this FA Cup fifth-round clash between Second Division Everton and top-flight opponents Manchester United will remember it as Dave Hickson's greatest hour.

Everton's swashbuckling centre-forward scored the winning goal with blood streaming down his face from a deep cut above his eyebrow. He had sustained the injury just before half-time and at that stage it looked as if he would be struggling to continue.

But spilling blood for his beloved Everton was all in a day's work for Hickson. Twice the referee asked him to go off. Twice the Blues' number nine shook his head and launched himself back into the fray. His courage would

eventually be rewarded in a quite remarkable game.

The Goodison pitch looked in fine condition for this clash, although the surface was just a little bit greasy, suggesting the turf might cut up as the game progressed.

At first sight, the crowd looked to be approaching the 70,000 mark. There were frustrating scenes on the Bullens Road side of the ground where many unlucky ticket holders did not get in until at least 25 minutes after the start although they were outside the ground in good time.

The trouble was caused by a terrific crush of people hoping to get into the paddock which was pay-at-the-gate. A mass of supporters jammed the north end of Bullens Road and the police, operating on foot, were powerless to do anything about it.

Even when the paddock turnstiles

were closed, people with tickets still could not force their way through. Eventually mounted police managed to sort things out, but by now the tie was well underway.

Peter Farrell won the toss and elected to defend the Gwladys Street End. United were the reigning Champions and clear favourites to win the game. The Manchester side featured stars like Ray Wood, Roger Byrne and David Pegg, but there was experience amongst them as well in the shape of Arthur Rowley and Johnny Carey, a man who would later change sides and manage the Blues.

United attacked with confidence early on and it was no surprise when they secured the lead after 27 minutes. Berry, with plenty of space on the right, out-foxed Lindsay with a feint to centre. Instead, he turned inside and beat his man before trying a shot which O'Neill parried. The rebound went straight to Rowley, who lashed it home from close range.

The Blues refused to lie down and two fine efforts from Buckle raised the home morale. The home side's fighting qualities came to the fore when Eglington equalised in the 34th minute. Cummins had made a clever pass to Hickson in the outside-right position. He quickly moved it on to Eglington, who rounded defender Aston and scored with a solid right-foot shot from ten

Dave Hickson was the hero of Goodison on 14 February 1953 when Second Division Everton knocked Champions Manchester United out of the FA Cup with a 2-1 victory. Hickson finished the tie covered in blood after sustaining a deep cut above his eyebrow, but he continued to head the ball bravely and scored a crucial goal. He is pictured challenging United's Ray Wood for a high ball.

yards out. It was his fifth goal in as many games.

Everton's elation was tempered by an injury to Hickson sustained just before half-time. The Goodison number nine took a nasty knock in the face and was led from the field with blood pouring from a badly cut eyebrow. It looked as if he might struggle to continue, let alone play a leading part in the second-half action.

But this was Dave Hickson, a real-life 'Roy of the Rovers'. He returned to the fray with a vengeance, shrugging the referee aside when he suggested a possible early retirement. United refused to give the Everton hero an inch, but then Davey never sought any favours.

The 'Football Echo' reported: *When Hickson was harrassed by two defenders as he tried to bore his way through, he was brought down by Carey and adopted a rather truculent attitude on getting up!*.

Truculent? The Cannonball Kid was spitting blood and breathing fire at the same time.

Ignoring his injured eye, he met a corner with his head and the ball thudded against an upright. Hickson was like a boxer who had taken a left hook, his eyebrow bursting open once more with the impact of the ball. The referee stopped the game, indicating that the player should now heed his advice and call it a day. Hickson, with the crowd roaring his name, simply trotted back into position.

Everton were now well on top. Farrell set up Eglington and the fans gasped as his superb lob sailed narrowly over the bar. United's Rowley and home full-back Clinton clashed and tempers were now getting a bit frayed to say the least.

Parker missed a golden opportunity to put the Blues in front when he screwed a left-foot shot well wide from an outstanding position, but it didn't matter.

Everton grabbed the lead after 63 minutes with a goal as dramatic as anything that had been scored on this famous ground, apart from Dixie's legendary 60th. Inevitably, Hickson was the name on the lips of every single member of the blue and white army.

He had played the half with blood pouring from that gash above his eye. The worse it got, the more determined Davey seemed to become. His golden moment began with a long ball from Clinton near the halfway line. Eglington claimed it and wasted no time at all in squaring it to Hickson.

Two defenders were tracking the Blond Bomber and he seemed to have little chance of making anything of the situation. But chasing the ball, he beat one man, side-stepped the other and then screwed back an angled shot that the despairing Wood failed to reach.

The crowd went wild. Hickson's grit and determination had won the day. One side of his face was a mass of red. The top half of his blue shirt had turned scarlet. But the man was still a tower of strength. He left the field to a standing ovation. Was such a salute ever more deserved?

Everton: O'Neill; Clinton, Lindsay, Farrell, T.E. Jones, Lello, Buckle, Cummins, Hickson, Parker, Eglington. *Attendance: 77,902*

Factfile: Everton met Aston Villa in the sixth round at Villa Park. Once again, Hickson was the man of the moment, scoring the only goal of the game to earn the Blues a semi-final challenge against Bolton Wanderers. It proved to be a sensational match, Parker (two) and Farrell scoring in a heartbreaking 4-3 defeat.

Bolton went on to lose at Wembley to Blackpool in what will forever be known as the Stanley Matthews Final. If the Blues had gone all the way, would the Cannonball Kid have stolen the Wizard of the Wing's thunder? Such dreams are what the Cup is all about. It's enough to say that Hickson had a season Evertonians will never forget.

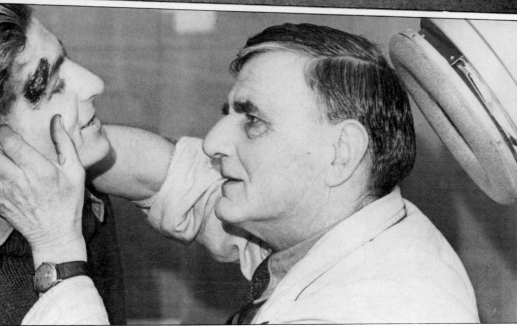

Three famous FA Cup goals en-route to the 1953 semi-final. Top: John Willie Parker scores in the 4-1 win over Nottingham Forest. Middle: Dave Hickson's memorable strike against Manchester United. Bottom: Hickson's quarter-final winner against Aston Villa.

The face of a battered hero. Dave Hickson has his badly gashed right eyebrow examined by trainer Harry Cooke after the sensational 1953 FA Cup victory over Manchester United.

The power and determination of Dave Hickson is captured perfectly in this photograph, a flying header at Goodison which produced an outstanding goal during the 1953-54 campaign.

A soccer giant at Goodison. The great John Charles of Leeds United gets in a solid header, challenged by Don Donovan in November 1953. The Blues won 2-1.

A fine action shot of Wally Fielding – a key figure in the 1954 promotion side. Fielding was a superb ball-playing inside-forward.

Sprinting back to the top . . .Dave Hickson, Eglington, Farrell and Parker prepare for a return to the First Division in the summer of 1954.

The players that took Everton back to the top flight in 1954: Back row (left to right): Moore, Farrell, T.E.Jones, O'Neill, Donovan, Lello, C.Leyfield (trainer). Front: Wainwright, Fielding, Hickson, Parker, Eglington.

Heading Back To The Big Time

Saturday, 24 April 1954

Everton 1 Birmingham City 0

EVERTONIANS approached the end of the 1953-54 season with just one thought in mind. The Second Division was no place for one of the greatest clubs in the land. After close on three years in the wilderness, enough was enough.

When Birmingham City visited Goodison Park for the final home League game of the season, victory was not so much important as absolutely crucial. A crowd of over 62,000 converged on the ground, each and every one of them hoping that the Blues

would overcome their promotion jitters. They had drawn the previous two games, both away from home, allowing Fulham (0-0) and Lincoln City (1-1) to share the spoils.

Birmingham were a more than useful side and there was an air of tense excitement about the crowd as they greeted their heroes with a deafening roar. The pitch had been well watered by the groundstaff and there was little doubt that the ball would zip up off the surface.

The visitors mounted two early attacks, clearly more relaxed than their opponents. The only thing the Birmingham players were playing for was their £2 win bonus. There was so much

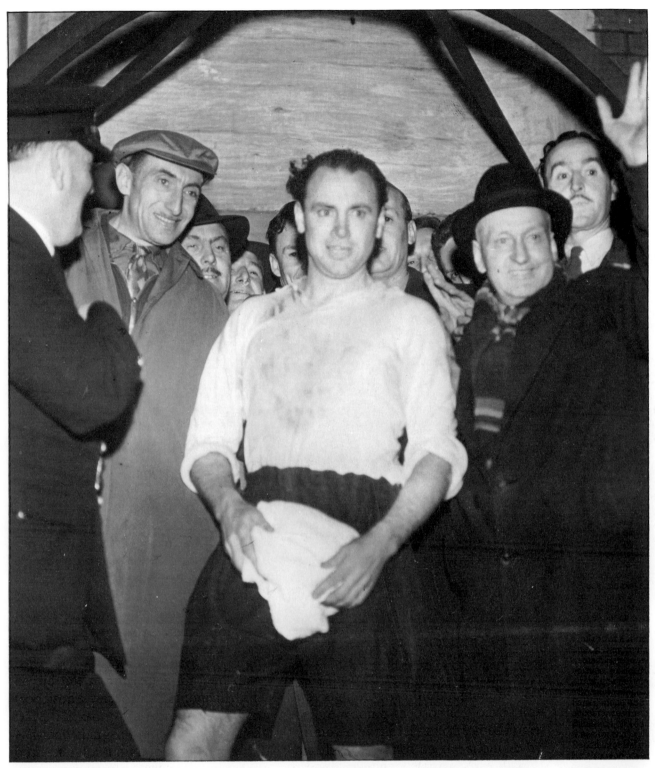

more at stake for Everton. Wally Fielding took a knock in the back although he did not require attention and then Goodison's very own Cannonball Kid, Dave Hickson, was grounded when Newman charged him as they disputed possession for a high lob.

The powerhouse centre-forward would eventually have the last word. Defenders found to their cost that Hickson was not a man to trifle with. The blond number nine was spoken to

by the referee for a foul on Newman just inside the Everton half. The official took the battling Blues' star to one side, waving away two Birmingham players before reading the riot act. Davey was unmoved by the ref's outstretched finger and he was patted on the shoulder by his skipper Peter Farrell.

The skirmish between striker and defender would turn into something of a war, but this was par for the course for Goodison idol Hickson.

Elation for Everton's sturdy wing-half and captain Peter Farrell at the end of the promotion-winning 1953-54 campaign. Farrell made 453 appearances for the Blues and played 28 times for the Republic of Ireland. He also won seven caps for Northern Ireland at a time when they could select Eire-born players for the Home International Championships.

121

A couple of minutes later Everton got a free-kick for a foul on Hickson by Newman. Then came a spell of incessant attacking by the home side with no end product. John Willie Parker was just too slow to take advantage of a short pass by Hickson in the vicinity of the six-yard box.

At this stage, the home side were not producing the dominance and combination in attack their fans had hoped for. Fielding and Parker were not making their usual good use of the ball and the crowd were getting a little bit restless until Hickson finally made the all-important breakthrough after 38 minutes.

Cyril Lello and Farrell linked to provide Tommy Eglington with a chance to get in a telling centre, but the resulting cross was too near the goalkeeper. Merrick double-fisted the ball away, but Hickson was hovering in a dangerous position and he rammed the ball back towards the net with a header that was almost as powerful as any shot.

The crowd erupted to salute their goal hero, who modestly waved back, his 24th League goal of the season in the bag.

Everton's opening home game on returning to Division One in 1954 was against a formidable Arsenal side. Tommy Eglington stepped in to head a brilliant winner in front of 69,000 delighted Evertonians.

There was an unusual incident in the second half when Hickson and Lello both went down after being charged by defenders. While the referee went to assess these painful knocks on the edge of one area, play continued just outside the area at the other end of the field. The fans screamed at the startled official who wheeled around and finally stopped play.

It helped to ease the tension and the Blues were soon celebrating a crucial victory that would take them into their final game at Oldham with the First Division beckoning them.

Everton: O'Neill; Moore, Donovan, Farrell, T.E. Jones, Lello, Wainwright, Fielding, Hickson, Parker, Eglington. *Attendance: 62,965*

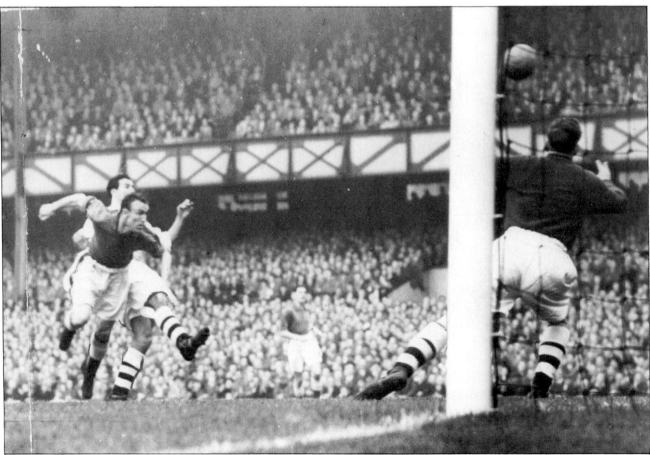

122

The Goodison fans idolised Dave Hickson. He had two spells with the Blues in the 1950s, playing for Aston Villa and Huddersfield in between. There was uproar when Everton sold the forceful centre-forward to Liverpool in November 1959.

Toffee Lady in the mid-1950s . . .Mary Gorry.

Lighting Up Goodison Park

Saturday, 9 October 1957

Everton 2 Liverpool 0

OVER 58,000 fans turned up at Goodison Park on 9 October 1957, for an historic occasion, Everton's first ever floodlit match.

The Blues were by no means pioneers in this field. Sheffield Wednesday, for instance, had installed a highly effective system at Hillsborough. And even non-League South Liverpool, very much Mersey minnows, had stolen a march on their famous neighbours. As early as September 1949, South had staged a floodlit game at their Holly Park ground against a Nigerian touring XI, attracting crowd of 13,000 people.

But there was no disputing the fact

FA Cup fever gripped Goodison in January 1955, when the Blues were drawn at home to Liverpool in the fourth round. Mounted police had to disperse a vast crowd in Goodison Road when tickets ran out. The queue had stretched for over a mile, many people having waited throughout the night. Sadly, Everton crashed 4-0 to their arch-rivals.

that the Goodison venture was both ambitious and highly effective. There was much hype about the new technology prior to the game. It was said that enough electricity to last an ordinary house for six months would be used in just one game.

Four giant pylons, each 185 feet high and operating initially with 36 lamps each, towered over the pitch, one in each corner of the ground. The towers, the tallest in the country, could accommodate a further 18 lamps on each pylon if it was felt that the illumination generated was insufficient.

The company installing the system claimed that each lamp would last for at least 500 hours, or 330 matches! At 25 shillings (£1.25p) a time, the bulbs were not deemed to be costly and to save spasmodic replacement, the makers suggested the club install new lamps every three to four years.

The lights themselves were 1,500-watt tungsten bulbs, each over a foot long and 15 inches in diameter. They screwed into their sockets, the illumination being heightened by huge concave mirrors behind each unit.

It was claimed that the light output was the equivalent of 400 good-sized houses blazing away with every light they had. The towers themselves were built to withstand hurricane-force winds of up to 120 mph. They could take a three-inch sway at the top, but the people who had scaled the towers during the weeks building up to the big switch-on claimed it felt more like three feet when a gust struck a pylon.

In truth, they were rock-solid, soaring so high that they were visible for miles around. Merseyside and North Wales Electricity Board officials had to build a special transformer sub-station to provide the necessary 6,000-volt load.

Everton cashed in on the system to electrically heat the water for the players' baths as well as installing an electric laundry. Would the team now provide some electrifying football?

All was revealed when the Blues entertained Liverpool on the big night for what was an extra-special occasion. It was not a League game, but rather

a first leg of the Liverpool County FA Anniversary Cup.

The Reds dominated in the opening half hour, but their finishing was erratic. They missed the all-round ability of Billy Liddell in the middle and the ball-control and scheming of Jimmy Melia. Equally, they had the misfortune of having a goal disallowed on the stroke of half-time for offside. Rowley looked 'on' when Molyneux booted the ball into the penalty area from the halfway line. The forward rounded Donovan and flicked the ball into the net, almost out of the hands of goalkeeper Dunlop.

But the flag was up and it meant Everton took advantage. They grabbed a two-goal lead early in the second half, both goals being scored by young Eddie Thomas who came on as a substitute for Fielding.

To add insult to injury, Liverpool claimed Everton's second goal was well offside, surrounding the referee and holding up the restart for over a minute. Hickson was yards 'off' when the movement began, but he was played on when the pass to him struck Byrne. Hickson ran on 20 yards before squaring the ball to the in-running Thomas to slot home.

The night was significant in as much as Liverpool gave a debut on the left wing to a young local boy, John Morrissey. He was their best forward in the first period, sending over some first-class centres. Morrissey, of course, would eventually cross the park for a bargain-fee of £10,000 in 1962 and become a firm Goodison favourite for close on a decade.

It was an illuminating night all round. Floodlit football would become part and parcel of life on Merseyside in the years that followed, but the people in Goodison Park that October night were very much in on the start of something big.

Everton: Dunlop; Donovan, Tansey, Birch, Jones, Meagan, McNamara, Temple, Hickson, Fielding(Thomas), Williams.
Attendance: 58,771

Floodlights were installed at Goodison Park in October 1957. Here is a worm's eye view of one of the towering pylons, rising behind Dave Hickson as he scores his second and Everton's third in a 3-1 victory over Birmingham City in 1958.

Carey Takes A Taxi Ride — And The 'Millionaires' Take Centre Stage

WHEN an Everton manager is under threat, you will hear the Goodison fans talking about the possiblity of him 'taking a taxi'. This phrase will totally bemuse outsiders, but Blues' fans are very much aware of its significance. In the summer of 1961, boss Johnny Carey travelled to London for a routine Football League meeting in tandem with club chairman John Moores.

Carey had been at the helm since 1958, a former Manchester United player who had learned the managerial ropes at Blackburn Rovers. Carey knew his football, of that there was no doubt. He brought the likes of Billy Bingham, Jimmy Gabriel, Roy Vernon and Alex Young to Goodison and in 1960-61 achieved fifth position in the First Division, the club's best placing since the war. The manager was on the right lines, but the man at the top, chairman Moores, was impatient for success. Head of the Littlewoods Organisation and Everton's chief shareholder, Moores was ready to use his vast fortune to help the Blues live up to their motto: 'Only The Best Will Do'.

Carey was calm, assured and extremely likeable, but the chairman wanted a strict disciplinarian at the helm, someone who would move ruthlessly in the transfer market to give the Blues that extra lift towards the top. And so when he left that fateful League meeting with Carey in tow, he chose to use the taxi journey to the station to inform his manager that his services would no longer be required.

To this day, struggling Everton managers dread the cry from the terraces of 'Take a taxi'. Carey took the 'sacking' decision with dignity, but it was nevertheless a shattering blow. Moores now appointed Sheffield Wednesday's Harry

An intriguing photograph of Everton manager Harry Catterick and chairman John Moores with a group of Everton apprentice professionals in November 1962, all schoolboy internationals. Left to right: Ken Griffiths, Aiden Maher, Geoff Harcombe, John Hurst, Gerry Humpheys, Geoff Barnett and Gerry Glover. All except Griffiths and Harcombe would play for the first team. It was said that Catterick only wore a tracksuit when Moores was about to make a visit. The 'Cat' had obviously had advance notice on this day!

Catterick to the hot seat, a man who had played centre-forward for Everton in the late 1940s and 1950s without setting the place alight. But if Catterick was only an average player, he was most certainly an outstanding manager.

With Moores' full support, he won the League Championship in his second season with a side packed full of riches. Everton were known universally at that time as 'The Millionaires'. It was a tag which was fully justified because Catterick made a string of big-money buys. But the end justified the means because the Blues would also win the FA Cup in 1966 before the manager

went off on a fresh tangent, building a new Championship side around home-grown players in 1969-70.

Throughout this period, the Moores influence was considerable. He was chairman twice, 1960-1965, and 1972-73. His success — first and foremost as a highly successful businessman and secondly as a leading figure in the world of sport (he also owned the old Liverpool Stadium boxing venue and was a leading shareholder in Liverpool Football Club) — earned him civic and national recognition. Moores was made an Honorary Freeman of the City in 1970, awarded the CBE in 1972 and was knighted in 1980, not least for his charitable services. In the same way that it is impossible to write about Everton without making mention of the likes of George Mahon and Will Cuff, those early Goodison guiding lights, it is impossible to talk about the modern Blues without making due reference to Sir John Moores. He exerted a very different type of influence, but it was nevertheless a crucial involvement, coming at exactly the right time.

Obviously, success is all about having the right players, but if a club has not got leadership from the top, mediocrity will always prevail. On the subject of managers, Everton's first recognised 'boss' was Theo Kelly, appointed to the post in 1939. Prior to that time, team selection was a matter for directors, specially appointed committees and senior coaches. Kelly had been club secretary for some years prior to being offered the new title of team manager. He would retain the position for seven years. He found himself in charge of a team playing wartime regional football in the first instance. Seemingly reluctant to move in the transfer unless it was absolutely vital, he angered the fans by selling Tommy Lawton to Chelsea in 1945 and the restless Joe Mercer to Arsenal. Some felt that his administrative background as secretary made him too careful in a financial sense.

He was finally replaced by Cliff Britton in 1948. Britton had been a stylish and highly respected wing-half with the club, gaining an FA Cup winners' medal alongside Dixie Dean and the rest in 1933. He had gained managerial experience with Burnley, taking them from the Second Division to the First as well as reaching an FA Cup Final.

An easy going, yet confident man, he took Everton to the 1950 FA Cup semi-final, a bitter losing experience against Liverpool. Things now took a sharp downwards turn and despite signing Harry Potts from Burnley and Jock Lindsay from Glasgow Rangers, the Blues suffered the indignity of being relegated for only the second time in their history in 1951. Britton now set about the challenge of restoring the club's top-flight status and after finishing seventh and 16th, Everton finally bounced back in 1953-54 as Second Division runners-up.

Britton stepped down in 1956 and for two years, the Blues had Ian Buchan operating, not as a manager in the true sense, but rather as first-team coach. Buchan was a fitness fanatic and he marshalled the Blues well in this respect, but he was no tactician and no one was surprised when Johnny Carey took over in 1958. Carey's rise and fall has been described earlier in this chapter, likewise the arrival of Catterick. 'The Cat' would put Everton back on the map in no uncertain terms with players of the calibre of Gordon West, Tommy Wright, Howard Kendall, Colin Harvey, Brian Labone, John Hurst, Johnny Morrissey and Joe Royle, to name just a few. Catterick won two Championships and the FA Cup between 1961 and 1973 when he 'moved upstairs' in an advisory capacity after suffering a heart attack. The great Everton manager died at Goodison Park after watching an FA Cup quarter-final against Ipswich Town on 9 March 1985.

Everton, having won the title in 1970 with what should have been the team of the decade, now inexplicably fell from grace. They went 13 long years without a major trophy, even though Billy Bingham, in the first instance, and then Gordon Lee would both go tantalisingly close. But John Moores, all those years earlier, had emphasised that he wasn't interested in Nearly Men. And so Howard Kendall accepted the call to Goodison in 1981 to become the most successful Everton manager of all time. Kendall was a class act as a player, a man whose powerhouse tackling and superb passing qualities helped to inspire that famous 1970 Championship success. Now, after a tense settling in period, he would win two titles in his own right, the FA Cup, the European Cup-winners' Cup and two Manager of the Year awards. He shocked the fans by leaving the club after the 1987 title success to join Athletic Bilbao with his right-hand man, Colin Harvey, taking charge. The old partnership was restored when Kendall returned in 1991, via Manchester City, with the joint aim once again to put the Blues back on top.

Johnny Carey was Everton manager between 1958 and 1961. He was sacked in a famous incident in the back of a taxi after leaving a League meeting in London with chairman John Moores. This photograph was taken in August 1959, Carey watching Dunlop, Ashworth, B.Harris, Tansey and Jones go through their paces at Bellefield. Managers in those days, of course, wore suits, not tracksuits.

Derek Temple's famous 1966 FA Cup Final goal against Sheffield Wednesday earned him a place in the Everton Hall of Fame. But Derek was rattling them in for the Blues long before that. He is pictured here in October 1957, rifling home the equaliser in a 1-1 draw with Burnley.

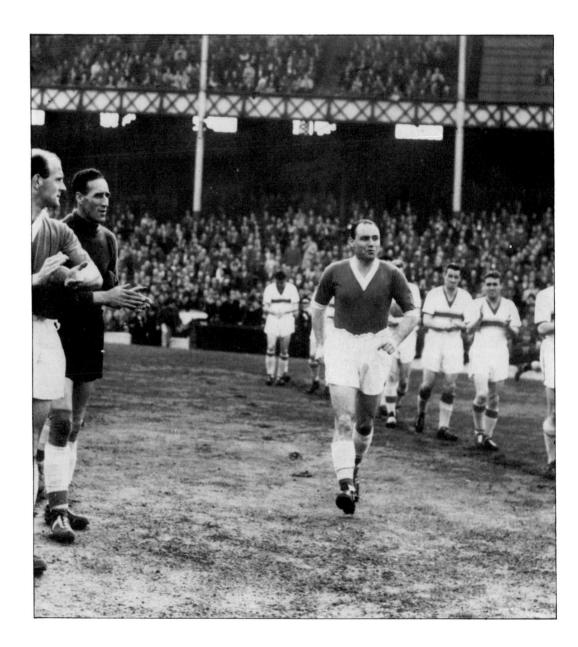

May 1960 and Peter Farrell figures in his last game as player-manager of Tranmere Rovers in the Liverpool Senior Cup Final at Goodison. Farrell had been an influential Everton captain in the 1950s. He is applauded on to the Goodison pitch he had graced so many times.

Harry Catterick inherited some good players from the sacked Johnny Carey in 1961. Billy Bingham, Bobby Collins, Alex Young, Roy Vernon and Jimmy Fell are pictured in training prior to the January 1962 FA Cup clash at Goodison with non-League King's Lynn. The Blues won 4-0. Remarkably, Bingham, Collins, Fell and Vernon – four of the men pictured – scored the goals.

The Golden Vision in full flight. Alex Young leaps over the despairing challenge of Cardiff City centre-half Danny Molloy in April 1961. Everton won 5-1, Young scoring two and Bobby Collins a hat-trick.

133

Everton's 'Little General' Bobby Collins was a bundle of dynamite for the Blues in 147 appearances, scoring 48 goals. He left Goodison for Leeds in 1962 and is seen here waving goodbye at Lime Street Station. He proved as inspirational at Elland Road as he had been at Goodison, being named Footballer of the Year in 1965.

Opposite page: A nice action shot of goalkeeper Albert Dunlop, who made 231 appearances between 1956 and 1963.

Three heads are better than one . . .Brian Harris, Jimmy Gabriel and Brian Labone leap in the snow in a 1961 training stint.

Opposite page, top: Alex Young wasn't very tall, but he had a tremendous spring. Here he challenges Manchester United goalkeeper Gaskell for a high centre in April 1962, a 1-1 draw.

Opposite page, bottom: September 1962, and the Everton squad with genuine title ambitions. Harry Catterick's car licence plate was 1 EFC.

The title beckons in May 1963. Everton beat Bolton 1-0 at Goodison with only three games left. Roy Vernon, the scorer, is seen testing Eddie Hopkinson who managed to deflect this shot wide.

Vernon Makes It V-Day

Saturday, 11 May 1963

Everton 4 Fulham 1

MANAGER Harry Catterick picked up an interesting Christmas present in December 1962. It was a new licence plate with the legend 1 EFC.

It was his way of saying that there was only one team in the country worth following in the ensuing months. Harry knew what he was talking about. Because on Saturday, 11 May 1963 the Blues stood on the verge of their first League Championship success since season 1938-39.

Fulham arrived on Merseyside like lambs to the slaughter. Everton needed two points to make certain of that title crown and nothing was going to stop them in that final game of the season.

Tottenham, chasing the Blues all the way, had sent a message to their London rivals suggesting that a little bit of capital pride would not go amiss. But the Merseysiders — and skipper Roy Vernon in particular — were to prove unstoppable.

Naturally, there was a certain amount of tension before the kick-off. Full-back Alex Parker recalls that Tony Kay tried to hide his nerves by singing as loudly

as he could. Vernon was cracking jokes non-stop, while Alex Young just sat there saying absolutely nothing.

Catterick's men had finished the season at a sprint. Prior to the Fulham clash they had won six of their previous eight games, drawing the other two at home. In doing so, they had overtaken Tottenham and Leicester in the race for the line. Now they stood just 90 minutes from glory.

Fulham, though, could not be ignored. Their side featured top-class goalkeeper Tony Macedo, England's first £100 a week footballer Johnny Haynes and former England international wing-half Bobby Robson. As it turned out, all the stars on the day were wearing royal blue shirts.

'Liverpool Echo' reporter Michael Charters summed up the scenes at Goodison perfectly in the wake of a resounding 4-1 victory, inspired by a Vernon hat-trick. He wrote: *Has there ever been an atmosphere, an excitement, a thrill sports-wise in Liverpool to equal that at Goodison?*

Old-timers, having seen the great football moments in this city over the past four decades, say there has been nothing like it since Dixie Dean broke the goalscoring record in 1928 in the last match of the season on the same pitch.

Over 60,000 delirious fans saluted the Blues on the final whistle and there were roars of laughter when a loudspeaker announcement, in giving the results of the Tottenham and Leicester games, commented: "Now let's see who could be the runners-up!"

Everton won the game with an outstanding first-half display. They were two up inside eight minutes, thanks to the accurate shooting of the matchless Vernon. The first came when he won possession on the ege of the area, speeding on to draw out Macedo before beating him with his swerve and pace — slotting an angled shot into the back of the net.

Fulham were soon reeling. Vernon chased an Alex Parker clearance with defender Mullery ahead of him and favourite to touch the ball back to his goalkeeper. Instead, the player struck the ball too hard and it rebounded off the 'keeper into the path of the marauding Vernon. He drew Macedo over to the right before scoring from almost the same position as the first goal.

Alex Young, Everton's acclaimed

Harry Catterick left the Championship celebration dinner in 1963 to drive north of the border and capture Partick Thistle's Sandy Brown for £38,000. Brown played in every position for the Blues, even taking the goalkeeper's jersey on one occasion when Gordon West was sent off. But Sandy scored a famous own-goal in a derby game against Liverpool and even now local Sunday League players are likely to refer to an 'og' as a 'Sandy Brown'.

How the title was won. This 1963 'Liverpool Echo' cartoon strip tells the story of the final day.

ENING EXPRESS, MONDAY, MAY 13, 1963

EVERTON v FULHAM.

THE ATMOSPHERE WAS ELECTRIC. THIS WAS A PRETTY GOOD THING, BECAUSE IT GALVANISED ROY VERNON INTO SCORING VERY QUICKLY.

ALMOST IMMEDIATELY HE GOT ANOTHER HANDY 230 VOLTS AND A SECOND GOAL.

HELPED BY TONY MACEDO PRESSING THE WRONG SWITCH.

THEN IT WAS FULHAM'S TURN TO PROVIDE A SHOCK —

BUT ALEX SCOTT, WIRED FOR POWER, MADE IT 3-1 —

— AND VERNON STEPPED UP THE VOLTAGE WITH A FOURTH GOAL. THE RESULTING UPROAR —

— COMPLETELY FUSED 60,000 SETS OF TONSILS, KILLED TWO BLACK-BACKED GULLS AND CAUSED A MAN TO FALL OFF HIS BIKE IN CONNAH'S QUAY

IN SALUTING ROY VERNON AND HIS TEAM.—

CONGRATULATIONS EVERTON, ON YOUR LEAGUE CHAMPIONSHIP!

NO GOALS, FEW THRILLS

Golden Vision, was having a wonderful match. His heading, distribution and artistry had the visitors in all kinds of trouble. But Fulham managed to reduce the arrears when Haynes and Robson linked superbly to enable outside-right Key to volley past Albert Dunlop, an end of season deputy for the injured Gordon West.

But with Tony Kay and Jimmy Gabriel moving forward at every opportunity to support the attack, Everton were soon pounding the Fulham defence once more. Dennis Stevens had the ball in the net from a clever Young header, but the referee had blown moments earlier for a foul by Keetch on Young.

It didn't matter because the Blues promptly scored from the resulting free-kick. Vernon's initial shot rebounded to Alex Scott and his low shot struck a Fulham player en-route to the back of the net to make it 3-1. The fans were breathless, having witnessed four goals in 28 minutes. It would be five minutes from time before Fulham were finally finished off.

A long clearance from Dunlop was headed through by the immaculate Young. Vernon once again beat Mullery in a close challenge for the ball, drew Macedo to the right and then sent an angled shot through the narrow gap into the corner of the net. The Championship celebrations now began in earnest.

A ring of policemen ensured there would be no wholesale pitch invasion. It meant the team could make the traditional lap of honour, cheered every inch of the way. The 'Liverpool Echo' reported that it was shattering, ear-shaking approval for the Everton team and management who had come through in the home straight to take 20 out of the last 24 points.

Having saluted the players, the fans now turned their attention to the directors' box, chanting: "We want John Moores."

The chairman had lost his hat when he threw it high in the air after Everton's second goal. He acknowledged the cheers and then the players joined him in the Main Stand, still in their playing strip, but clutching bottles of champagne. Tony Kay, all dash and power and aggression on the pitch, was puffing on a giant cigar, the kind Winston Churchill would have been proud of.

The crowd were delighted and only calmed down long enough for skipper Vernon to make a short speech. The mutual respect between players and fans was there for all to see. It was time for everyone to wend their way home, manager Catterick climbing into his car, registration number 1 EFC.

It was a four-wheeled League table, a Champion Chariot. The 'Cat' was the proudest man in England.

Everton: Dunlop; Parker, Meagan, Gabriel, Labone, Kay, Scott, Stevens, Young, Vernon, Temple.

Attendance: 60,578

Tony Kay was a red-haired tiger who cost Everton £55,000 when they signed him from Sheffield Wednesday in November 1962. He immediately helped to inspire a Championship success, but found himself caught up in a major soccer bribes scandal in 1965, linked with his Hillsborough days. He was subsequently banned for life.

Everton's 1963 Championship captain Roy Vernon with another Goodison title-winning skipper, the legendary Dixie Dean.

Far right: The 1962-63 title is in the bag and Harry Catterick toasts the crowd in champagne from the Main Stand. Tony Kay, by his side, is smoking a big cigar. The rest celebrate in a more straightforward manner, including Jimmy Gabriel, Derek Temple, Albert Dunlop (deputising for the injured Gordon West), Brian Labone, Alex Parker, Alex Scott and Alex Young.

Everton crushed Manchester United 4-0 at Goodison to take the FA Charity Shield in 1963 with goals from Gabriel, Stevens, Temple and Vernon. A delighted Vernon holds up the Shield with John Moores.

Dennis Stevens was an ever-present in the 1962-63 title success. He is seen scoring in the subsequent FA Charity Shield victory over Manchester United at Goodison.

Milan Maestros Hit Town

Wednesday, 18 September 1963

Everton 0 Inter-Milan 0

EVERTON played in the Champions Cup for the first time in 1963 after an outstanding title-winning campaign on the home front. Their first opponents in the European Cup were famous Italians, Inter-Milan, who came to Goodison suggesting that their first-leg tactics would be based on out-and-out defence.

Legendary coach Helenio Herrera said as much in his pre-match Press conference, but it was nothing more than a clever confidence trick.

Milan stepped out in front of 62,000 fans to play a superb attacking game in the first half and while they packed their defence when they needed to, the emphasis was on swift and decisive attacking breaks that thrilled the crowd.

The Italians were precise in everything they did. Everton were never allowed to gain the upper hand and the resulting goalless draw suited the visitors down to the ground.

Inter had a magnificent centre-back in Guarneri and he overshadowed home favourite Alex Young, helped by deep-lying left-half Picchi. The numbers on the backs of the visiting defenders were meaningless. They move around fluently, plugging gaps and playing themselves out of trouble with a calm assurance and genuine skill. It was a highly impressive display.

World-renowned inside-left Suarez collected the ball from his defence and sent crisp, accurate passes cutting through the home defence. This free-flowing player stamped his authority on the game and earned the admiration of the appreciative Goodison fans. But the biggest danger came from flying winger Jair, who got more shots in than any other player. Brian Harris did well to contain him as much as he did.

For their part, Everton's forwards struggled to break down the solid Inter defence.

Everton met Italian giants Inter-Milan in the first round of the European Cup in September 1963. Roy Vernon goes close in the goalless first leg, but is thwarted by goalkeeper Sarti.

Inter Milan goalkeeper Sarti leaps high to deny Alex Young as he tried to reach a Jimmy Gabriel centre during the European Cup, first-round, first-leg game at Goodison in 1963. There was a major selection surprise in the return when a San Siro Stadium baptism of fire was handed to a young Colin Harvey. The Blues lost 1-0, but a famous Goodison career was underway.

The normally influential Roy Vernon failed to make an impact on the proceedings, shadowed constantly by right-half Tagnin. At the same time, wingers Derek Temple and Alex Scott were well-marshalled by Faccetti and Burgnich. Everton's only success story on the night was in defence where Brian Labone and Alex Parker played particularly well.

To be fair, Parker had no winger to mark and so effectively had the freedom of the field on the right. He was able to push well forward and produced Everton's best shot of the night. Jimmy Gabriel moved into the attack in the second half, but even his heading ability and thrust failed to trouble the Italians too much.

Tony Kay was full of fire and his tackling was ferocious at times. He had his name taken, apparently for treading on Suarez's hand.

Inter were given an ovation from the crowd at the end. They had almost stolen victory at the death when Suarez sent Jair racing through with a 40-yard pass. Only a last-ditch tackle by Harris saved the day.

Everton's failure to snatch a goal meant that the return in the imposing San Siro Stadium was virtually a foregone conclusion. But the Italians were quick to salute the Goodison crowd. One report said: *The way they sportingly applauded the Milan players at the end stamped them as real gentlemen.*

Everton: West; Parker, Harris, Gabriel, Labone, Kay, Scott, Stevens, Young, Vernon, Temple.
Attendance: 62,000

Factfile: Inter-Milan duly won the return 1-0. From Everton's point of view, the night was significant for one thing. A youngster named Colin Harvey was thrust into the San Siro cauldron and acquitted himself superbly. It was the start of a famous career for one of Goodison's favourite sons.

As the 1963-64 season drew to a close with a home game against West Ham, there was once again no place in the side for Goodison idol Alex Young. 'Sack Catterick, keep Young', was the message from one supporter who is led away by a policeman. Catterick seemed to be vindicated when Fred Pickering, wearing the Golden Vision's number nine shirt, scored twice in a 2-0 win. But 18 months later there would be a more serious sequel when Catterick was kicked by fans in a disgraceful incident at Blackpool after once again overlooking Young's claims. This time he had given a shock debut to a 16-year-old local boy, Joe Royle. Young would bounce straight back and go on to help Everton win the FA Cup that year, but it's worth noting that Royle eventually became one of the greatest Everton centre-forwards of all time.

Far left: Well done, Fred. In his first match for Everton, in March 1964, Fred Pickering scored a hat-trick. Alex Scott offers his congratulations at the end of the match against Nottingham Forest.

Left: Fred Pickering was a powerhouse centre-forward, signed by Everton from Blackburn in 1964. He scored a hat-trick on his England debut against the United States in a 10-0 victory, but was involved in a sensation in 1966 when he was left out of Everton's Cup Final side. As it turned out, the man who replaced him, Mike Trebilcock, proved to be a two-goal Wembley hero.

Below: It looks as if Liverpool's giant skipper Ron Yeats has delivered a karate chop to fell Everton's Alex Scott in this derby clash in February 1964. In fact, Scott had just shot narrowly wide in a 3-1 victory.

Roy Vernon was a lethal penalty-taker as Manchester United goalkeeper David Gaskell found to his cost in 1963-64.

The man signing out is Mick Meagan, bound for Huddersfield in July 1964. The man on the way in, standing, is England's Ray Wilson, who went on to play for England in the 1966 World Cup Final. He was possibly the greatest left-back Everton have ever had.

Little and Large, but no laughing matter . . .the clock shows 3.40pm and rival skippers Brian Labone and Leeds United's ex-Blue Bobby Collins walk from the Goodison pitch after the referee stopped an explosive game. Everton's Sandy Brown had been sent off after only four minutes. An Evertonian encroached on the pitch and had to be restrained by Johnny Morrissey as he exchanged angry words with Billy Bremner and Norman Hunter. Sanity eventually prevailed and play resumed, Leeds finishing 1-0 winners.

Opposite page, top: Jimmy Gabriel leaps above teammate Jimmy Husband to head Everton's equaliser in a 2-2 draw with Blackburn in October 1965.

Opposite page, bottom: An early goal from Jimmy Gabriel, Everton's powerhouse wing-half, helped inspire a 3-1 win over Spurs in October 1965.

Everton chairman Mr Holland Hughes met the players prior to the 1965-66 season and asked them to 'snooker' all-comers in the year ahead. Alex Young, Jimmy Gabriel and Brian Labone look on.

Everton beat Nuremberg 2-1 on aggregate in the first round of the 1965-66 Inter-Cities Fairs Cup. The team are pictured leaving for the airport from Goodison for the 1-1 first leg. Left to right: Fred Pickering and Johny Morrissey (on the bus), Dennis Stevens, Sandy Brown, Jimmy Gabriel, Derek Temple, Gordon West, Andy Rankin, Tommy Wright, Colin Harvey, Ray Wilson and a pipe-smoking Brian Harris. Note the ground entry price of four shillings (20p).

Opposite page, top: Cup training in January 1966, prior to the third-round clash with Sunderland. Leapfrog partners are Alex Young, Colin Harvey, Brian Harris, Brian Labone, Alex Scott, Sandy Brown, Derek Temple and Fred Pickering.

Opposite page, bottom: On the rails to FA Cup glory in 1966. Manager Harry Catterick and coach Tom Eggleston head for London with the team for the Final battle with Sheffield Wednesday.

Everton's FA Cup Final appearance in 1966 inspired this reunion of members of the 1933 Cup-winning side. Back (left to right): Jimmy Stein, Albert Geldard, Billy Cook, Jock Thomson. Front: Tommy White, Ted Sagar and Dixie Dean.

The FA Cup has been won in 1966 and the players parade the trophy along Scotland Road in an open-top bus.

155

A spectacular aerial shot of Goodison Park taken in conjunction with the 1966 World Cup. Work is being carried out on new staircases and facilities at the Stanley Park End.

World-Class Memories Of Pelé, Eusebio And Gallant North Korea

WHEN the World Cup Finals came to England in 1966, it went without saying that Goodison Park would be one of the venues. Brazil, Bulgaria, Hungary and Portugal featured in Group Three matches on Merseyside, and Goodison also staged a truly sensational quarter-final clash in which the gallant North Koreans played their part and the semi-final between the Soviet Union and West Germany.

These were exciting times for the soccer-mad public of Liverpool with legendary stars like Pelé and Eusebio treading a very impressive Goodison stage. The old Main Stand, with its vast standing enclosure below was an awe-inspiring sight when it was packed.

A feature that hits you when you view aerial pictures from 1966 is the presence of the two D-shaped safety rings behind each goal which prevented missiles being launched the way of unsuspecting goalkeepers. In the first instance there were three matches, each with a very special appeal.

World Champions Show Their Age

12 July 1966

Brazil 2 Bulgaria 0

BRAZIL, the pride of South America and the World Champions, were given Goodison Park as their base for their three opening matches, but the famous team was beginning to show its age.

Two stars of the 1958 World Cup winning team had been recalled in Orlando and Bellini. They joined vastly experienced individuals like Djalmar Santos and Garrincha in a side that was a strange mix of men possibly past their best linked with thrilling new talent. Of course, Pelé was a class act and there were others with wonderful ability, like Tostão, Gerson and flying winger Jairzinho.

No wonder the Merseyside fans flocked in their thousands to Goodison to see Brazil begin with a clash against Bulgaria. Alas, the cynicism of the Bulgarian defenders helped to ruin the game as a spectacle. Pelé was involved in a running battle with his marker Zhechev.

Instead of concentrating on his own strengths, the Brazilian ace allowed himself to be side-tracked and he was guilty of one or two niggling fouls of his own. In this tit-for-tat atmosphere, the Bulgarian was always going to have the final say and he cut down his opponent with a tackle that infuriated the 5,000 Brazilians in the crowd. Pelé, seen writhing in agony on the Goodison turf, would now miss the next match through injury.

Earlier, he had scored the first goal of the 1966 tournament when he bent a superb free-kick wide of Bulgarian

Everton's Main Stand, built in 1909, was described as one of the wonders of the sporting world. It was fronted by a vast enclosure for standing spectators, an area that swept back, under the elevated seating section.

July 1966 and the safety 'D' can clearly be seen behind the Gwladys Street goal to deter missile-throwing.

'keeper Naidenov. It was an historic moment, the player becoming the first player to score in three successive tournaments.

Garrincha was also playing in the Finals for the third time and he increased Brazil's lead after 63 minutes, also with a swerving free-kick. But despite their winning start, it was clear that this was not the Brazil of previous years.

Brazil: Gilmar; D.Santos, Bellini, Altair, Paulo Henrique, Denilson, Lima, Garrincha, Pele, Alcindo, Jairzinho.
Bulgaria: Naidenov; Shalamanov, Vutzov, Gaganelov, Penev, Kitov, Zhechev, Yakimov, Dermendyev, Asparoukhov, Kolev.
Attendance: 52,847

Hungary's first goal against Brazil at Goodison in 1966. Goalkeeper Gilmar is grounded, well beaten by Bene's shot.

Goodison Glory For Magical Magyars

15 July 1966

Hungary 3 Brazil 1

BRAZIL kicked-off their second Goodison game without Pelé, but they were able to replace him with the talented Tostão. The stylish Gerson also came into the side. The rain poured down on an overcast Merseyside afternoon, but the football was of the highest class.

Hungary's display was said to be reminiscent of the glory years of 1953 when they had the likes of Puskas and Hidegkuti in their ranks, players who had helped crush England for the first time at Wembley. The new Hungary had a real star in Florian Albert, whose running and passing had the Brazilians in all kinds of trouble.

Brazil were down after only three minutes when Bene claimed a loose pass, racing through to claim a fine goal. Tostão equalised after 14 minutes when a Lima free-kick rebounded to him, but Hungary carved open a superb chance after 63 minutes when Albert found

158

The World Cup Finals produced some magical moments at Goodison in 1966. Brazil's Jair gets in a flying header against Hungary, only for goalkeeper Gelei to save.

Farkas of Hungary raises his arms in delight after scoring his side's second against Brazil in a shock 3-1 1966 World Cup victory.

Bene and the winger crossed for Farkas to volley home.

Ten minutes from time, Meszoly converted a penalty to make it 3-1 and inflict upon Brazil their first World Cup defeat since 1954. The fans had turned up to Goodison to marvel at the Brazilians, but they went home saluting Albert & Co, and the magical Magyars.

Hungary: Gelei; Kaposzta, Matrai, Sipos, Szepesi, Mathesz, Meszoly, Bene, Albert, Farkas, Rakosi.
Brazil: Gilmar, D.Santos, Bellini, Altair, Paulo Henrique, Lima, Gerson, Garrincha, Alcindo, Tostão, Jairzinho.
Attendance: 57,455.

Champions — And Entertainers

November 1969, and Everton already lead the table with just one defeat in 17 games. They extended the run with a 1-0 home win over Forest. Jimmy Husband makes a spectacular leap over the fallen Hennessey. The ball rebounded off the Forest man and Tommy Wright plundered the match-winner.

Wednesday, 1 April 1970

Everton 2 West Brom 0

EVERTON clinched the Championship in style in a game in which they ran the show from midfield, inspired by the legendary Ball-Harvey-Kendall triumvirate. One could only feel sorry for Albion, who had to try and make a game of it in the emotion-charged atmosphere of Goodison Park.

The Blues performance was full of the brilliance that had mesmerised teams the length and breadth of the country in the preceding months. It was fitting that they should clinch the title in the last home game of the season, handing out a football lesson to their unfortunate rivals.

Everton produced two goals on the night, but it could so easily have been a bagful. John Osborne in the Albion goal had a splendid match, which was just as well for the outclassed visitors.

Harry Catterick's men took 13 minutes or so to settle down, clearly feeling the tension of the occasion. But they soon moved into overdrive and never looked back.

With total control in midfield, the Blues dominated for 90 per cent of the game. Johnny Morrissey, strong and direct on the left, had one of his best games of the season and ripped the Albion defence to shreds.

Alan Whittle defied his comparative inexperience with another dashing display of front running, getting on the scoresheet for the sixth successive game.

Joe Royle, a centre-forward in the finest Everton tradition, also played his part. Here was a team with class in every department.

Roger Kenyon was commanding at centre-back, doing a tremendous job in the continued absence of injured skipper Brian Labone. Tommy Wright and Sandy Brown were also comfortably in control on those rare occasions when Albion threatened.

And goalkeeper Gordon West, always a crowd favourite, only had one save to make, dealing superbly with an effort from Len Cantello. West was as much a spectator as anyone in the 58,523 crowd — the highest attendance of the season. This would be Everton's seventh successive win, giving them an unassailable nine points lead at the top of the table.

The game was played to a continuous roar of appreciation. it was a classical display of football, speedy, accurate and incisive. Colin Harvey almost scored in the opening moments, but Osborne, produced the first of a series of quality saves.

But he had no chance when Whittle broke the deadlock after 20 minutes with his 11th goal in 15 League games. Harvey tried to get in a shot from the edge of the area, but mis-hit the ball. Whittle seized control and kept a cool head, unleashing a fierce shot that struck a defender on the way into the roof of the net.

Harvey settled it midway through the half with one of the great goals of the season. The 'Liverpool Echo' reported: *He collected the ball way out, took it down the left, turned back in his tracks and lost two of his shadowers at the same time. He brought the ball into the middle and cracked in a shot from 25 yards which left the airborne Osborne helpless. What a goal to clinch the title.*

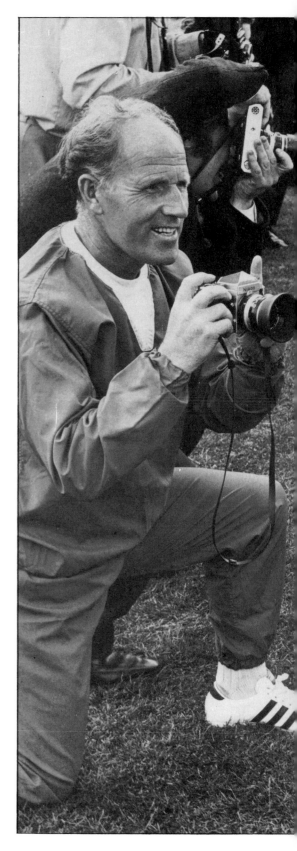

The scenes on the final whistle as Everton celebrated their seventh League Championship triumph were remarkable. Manager Catterick was first on to the pitch, throwing an arm around each player in turn as they headed for the dressing-room. With the volume of noise increasing by the second, the players returned for a lap of honour.

Labone, a reluctant spectator during the game itself, now joined his team-mates on the pitch and there was a special cheer for the injured skipper. Hundreds of fans now spilled onto the pitch despite appeals for them to remain on the terraces.

In July 1969, these Everton players were preparing for what would be one of the most famous Goodison seasons of all time. Coach Wilf Dixon has his Champions-elect in the picture, not least from the right: Roger Kenyon, Geoff Barnett, Howard Kendall, John Hurst, Brian Labone, Alan Whittle, Gordon West, Colin Harvey, Alan Ball, Tommy Wright, Tommy Jackson, Jimmy Husband and Gerry Humphreys.

The players disappeared to the safety of the dressing-room once more, but soon reappeared in the directors' box where Louis Edwards, chairman of Manchester United and a member of the League Management Committee, presented the trophy which had been collected in a secret trip to Leeds a couple of days earlier. Alan Ball, captain in Labone's absence, received the trophy from Mr Edwards.

Ball had been an inspirational figure throughout a memorable campaign, his competitive spirit, skill and never-say-die approach winning him an army of admirers.

This was the team that should have dominated English football for the next five years. That the side broke up without winning another major trophy remains one of the great mysteries of modern football.

But in 1969-70, Ball & Co reigned supreme, and on that April night, Goodison Park was the stage on which the finest team the Evertonians had seen for many a long year demonstrated that there is no substitute for class.

Everton: West; T.Wright, Brown, Kendall, Kenyon, Harvey, Whittle, Ball, Royle, Hurst, Morrissey.

Attendance: 58,523

Happiness is an FA Charity Shield victory over Chelsea in August 1970. Colin Harvey leads the celebrations after a 2-1 win. Howard Kendall and Alan Whittle were the scorers.

Germans Crushed In Penalty Shoot-Out

4 November 1970

Everton 1
Borussia Mönchengladbach 1
(Everton won on penalties)

EVERTON went into this European Cup, second-round return against Borussia Mönchengladbach, determined to prove their worth as English Champions, despite their disappointing form on the home front.

They had swept to the League Championship seven months earlier, playing football of the very highest class with the famous Ball-Harvey-Kendall midfield combination an inspirational force.

Harry Catterick's men now had the perfect opportunity to re-emphasise

A famous Goodison moment in the European Cup in November, 1970. Goalkeeper Andy Rankin punches the air after denying Borussia Mönchengladbach's Muller in a tense penalty shoot-out. His teammates leap for joy and the ground erupts with 42,000 celebrating victory.

their quality on a European stage, having held the German Champions to a 1-1 draw in the away leg with a crucial goal from Kendall.

Prior to this match, the legend persisted that the greatest game ever seen at Goodison was the 6-4 FA Cup replay victory over Sunderland on 30 January 1935. After a thrilling Champions Cup tie, there was a powerful school of thought that this game was the greatest of them all, certainly in terms of drama and nail-biting excitement.

The 42,744 fans lucky enough to be present witnessed a magnificent duel which ended with a thrilling penalty shoot-out in which Everton goalkeeper Andy Rankin was the hero of the hour. The Blues won the spot-kick battle 4-3 after the game had been drawn 1-1 (aggregate 2-2) after 30 minutes of extra-time.

The match began as sensationally as it finished with Morrissey claiming a goal after just 24 seconds. Borussia 'keeper Kleff completely misjudged an orthodox cross from the left winger, the ball skidding off the wet turf and finding the back of the net with the visiting defenders totally stunned.

It was the perfect start, but while Everton had most of the play, carving out chance after chance, the German 'keeper now made a mockery of his schoolboy error by producing a string of world-class saves.

Kleff made two spectacular back-breaking saves to deny Royle in the first half and his goalkeeping wizardry continued when he left Kendall, Morrissey, Husband and Harvey all cursing their luck.

Rankin had been little more than a spectator, but he lost possession after making a fine save from a Laumann header after 34 minutes and the German followed up to equalise on the rebound.

Everton now produced a great team display to try to find a way through with Kendall outstanding in terms of his

tackling and passing, Royle brilliant in the air and Hurst sound in central defence. Brown and Husband were brought on for the tiring Newton and Whittle to add some fresh zest in the final 30 minutes, but Borussia held on and the whole stadium held its breath as the penalty shoot-out now unfolded.

It started badly for the Blues. Royle, such a force in normal play, saw his kick saved by the inspirational Kleff, who had more than made amends for his earlier blunder. Sielhoff put the Germans ahead, only for Ball to make it 1-1.

Laumann, Borussia's goal hero, now held his head in his hands after pushing his penalty well wide and Everton were back on course. Morrissey put them in front, Heynckes made it 2-2 and Kendall, Koppel and Brown all converted to make it 4-3 with just one kick left.

By now the atmosphere was unbelievable. The whole ground was buzzing and the Goodison roar reached a crescendo as Muller, a great figure in the German defence, stepped up with the thankless task of trying to keep his side in the game. He hit the ball hard enough, but Rankin dived to his right to push the shot away and he was immediately engulfed by delighted team mates.

The fans were singing in the rain, ecstatic that their side had moved into the third round.

It had been a truly wonderful night and while it's nigh on impossible to say which was the greatest Goodison occasion of them all, this match would certainly take some beating in terms of a fever-pitch finish.

Everton: Rankin; Wright, K.Newton (Brown), Kendall, Kenyon, Harvey, Whittle(Husband), Ball, Royle, Hurst, Morrissey.

Everton's European Cup campaign in 1970 began with a home game against no-hopers Keflavik, who took a shock lead. But Alan Ball led a storming revival, claiming this cool equaliser and eventually completing his hat-trick in a 6-2 win. Royle (2) and Kendall also scored and a 3-0 away win increased the aggregate score to 9-2.

Gordon West was a brilliant shot-stopper and a magnificent character to have in the dressing-room. The Everton 'keeper is pictured in action against Sheffield United in August 1971.

Class on the field and a pretty smart team off it. Joe Royle, Henry Newton, Howard Kendall, Brian Labone and John Hurst attend a function in April 1971.

Alan Ball suggests to the photographers that the Blackpool goalkeeper's agony had absolutely nothing to do with him in a goalless draw, April 1971. Ball was a marathon man, a top-class goalscorer, a firebrand and an inspirational leader. Remember the famous white boots, mud-splattered in this instance.

Opposite page, top: Everton crushed Southampton 8-0 in a remarkable Goodison clash in November 1971. The Blues were snow kings for the day, not least Joe Royle who scored four. David Johnson got a hat-trick and Alan Ball completed the rout. Royle is seen causing havoc in the Saints' goal.

Opposite page, bottom: A fine action shot showing the shooting power of Howard Kendall as he scores in a 2-2 draw with Wolves in March 1972.

Colin Harvey had all the qualities of a top-class midfielder. He was supremely mobile, had vision and never shirked a tackle.

They used to say Mike Lyons would run through a brick wall for Everton. He never gave less than 100 per cent in over 400 appearances, switching comfortably between centre-half and centre-forward. He is pictured celebrating at David Webb's expense after scoring in a 2-0 win over Queen's Park Rangers in 1972.

Former Goodison right winger Billy Bingham returned as manager in the summer of 1973, faced with a major rebuilding job. He is pictured with chairman John Moores discussing the challenge.

Joe Harper joined Everton in December 1972, hailed as a new breed of striker. Only 5ft 6in tall, the former Aberdeen star relied on his sharpness in the box. He celebrates after scoring in a 3-0 win over Ipswich at the start of the 1973-74 season, but returned to Scotland after only 14 months at Goodison.

Gordon Lee left Newcastle United to replace Billy Bingham as Everton manager in January 1977. Lee was dedicated and hard-working but, like Bingham, failed to bring a major trophy to Goodison. He was replaced by Howard Kendall in 1981.

It looks as if Goodison has been bombed. In fact, it is a major demolition job to remove the remainder of the old Main Stand so that the new structure could be completed in 1971.

Latchford's £10,000 jackpot

Saturday, 29 April 1978

Everton 6 Chelsea 0

EVERTON finished the 1977-78 season with nothing to show in terms of silverware. But the final game of the season was an unforgettable occasion and not just because the Blues crushed Chelsea 6-0 in front of an ecstatic crowd of 40,000 people. It was also the day when Bob Latchford became the first top-flight player for six years to take his seasonal League tally to 30 goals.

The Evertonians turned up in force to see him plunder a memorable double and claim a £10,000 prize put up by the 'Daily Express' newspaper. The bounty added to the occasion, whipping the

fans up into a frenzy every time the home side moved on to the attack.

Latchford, a bustling centre-forward who was deadly in the box, will never forget the afternoon when Goodison Park went goal crazy and he was the toast of Merseyside.

He said: "There was quite an atmosphere that day, considering there wasn't very much on the game itself. The pitch was dry and bobbly, but the goals soon started to flow."

The one drawback was that the home side powered into a 3-0 lead without Latchford finding the net. Would he miss out on that lucrative cash bonanza? Bob provided the answer with a second half header that produced a deafening roar from the royal blue army, but he

Above, top: A typical Bob Latchford goal, plundered inside 90 seconds in a 4-0 win over Spurs in March 1977.

Above: Bob Latchford was at his best, poaching from close range. This is his 26th League goal of the season in his highly successful 1977-78 campaign, scored against Derby County.

The bearded Bob Latchford was an instant hit with the Evertonians in 1974. He is saluted here by the Goodison fans after scoring twice in a 4-1 win over his old club, Birmingham City.

was still one goal short of his target with the clock ticking away.

Everton conjured up goal number five, but the scorer was Mike Lyons, who vividly recalls the crowd's reaction.

He said: "I tucked the ball into the bottom corner and turned away to celebrate, but because I had failed to knock the ball back to 'Latch', who was in a great position, everybody just stood

and looked at me. It's the only time I've scored at Goodison and felt sick about it!''

But the man of the moment would not be denied his finest hour. His moment of glory came from the penalty spot and when the ball flew into the back of the net, the place erupted. He said: ''It was a terrific moment, a fantastic way to end a season.''

Naturally, everybody thought Latchford was in the money. In reality, his bank balance was boosted, only to the tune of £192. Part of the deal was that half of the £10,000 would go to the Football League and Professional Footballers' Association Benevolent Fund. Bob decided to share the rest with all of the players who had helped him achieve his 30-goal total. Hence, £10,000 became the princely sum of £192.

Even then, the story had a sting in the tail. Latchford was taxed on the basis that he had received a £5,000 bonus and it took him three years to sort the wrangle out with the Inland Revenue.

Still, Bob had taxed the resolve of defenders up and down the country during that free-scoring campaign. The only disappointment was that Everton only managed to finish third in the table when many people felt they were good enough that year to have gone all the way.

For the record, the goals against Chelsea that memorable April day were scored by Latchford (two), Dobson, Lyons, Robinson and Wright.

Everton: Wood; Robinson, Pejic, Lyons, Wright, Buckley, King, Dobson, Latchford, Telfer, Thomas.
Attendance: 39,504

Bob Latchford scored an impressive 138 goals in 286 full appearances for the Blues. Goodison fans will recall this celebratory pose.

Everton's 2-0 win over Stoke in March 1980 included Bob Latchford's 100th League goal. He turns to the crowd as his teammates celebrate while the electric scoreboard notes his memorable achievement.

An Evertonian Pizza Parlour manger, known locally as Rocco, was so convinced that Bob Latchford would score his 30th League goal of the 1977-78 season at Chelsea in the penultimate game that he said he would shave his head if it didn't happen. A bald Rocco is pictured looking distinctly glum. Latchford produced the goods a week too late to prevent this hair-raising story.

Duncan McKenzie was Everton's Mr Magic for two seasons in the late 1970s. Signed from Anderlecht, he had tremendous skill and was a real crowd pleaser.

Everton had the measure of arch-rivals Liverpool in this fourth-round FA Cup tie in January 1981. The Blues won 2-1 with goals from Peter Eastoe and Imre Varadi. Ray Clemence is in a tangle in the net as Varadi celebrates his goal.

Everton 1983-84; The team finished seventh that year, but reached the Milk Cup Final and won the FA Cup.

In Goodison Place for the first time. Andy Gray joined Everton in November, 1983 and made an immediate impact.

Peter Reid was a combative, inspirational figure for Everton in the 1980s. He is pictured here speaking on behalf of the injured Adrian Heath against Luton Town in April 1984.

Andy Gray scored spectacular goals. He is seen netting with a diving header in a 4-1 home win over Sunderland in 1985.

Left: A touch of class . . .Mrs Maguerite Murphy used to watch every single game at Goodison, first team, reserves and youth side. She also had a regular Monday lunch date at the Royal Blue Restaurant and got the surprise of her life in September, 1984, when her lunch companions turned out to be the FA Cup, Youth Cup and Charity Shield. She was absolutely delighted.

Right: The 1985 Everton Toffee Girl, Joanne Francis.

Gary Lineker was voted PFA Player of the Year at the end of his only Goodison season. He is pictured with manager Howard Kendall who, soon afterwards, would accept a massive Barcelona bid for the England star's signature.

Lineker's Goodison Swansong

5 May 1986

Everton 3 West Ham United 1

EVERTON wrapped up the 1985-86 season with a crushing 3-1 victory over West Ham United, inspired by a Gary Lineker double.

The fans in attendance that day could not have realised that they were watching the free-scoring striker in action in a blue shirt at Goodison Park for the very last time.

He would play and score in the FA Cup Final against Liverpool just days later, taking his tally for the season to 40 goals.

He would then head for Mexico with England for a World Cup challenge that would catapult him into an international spotlight and draw admiring glances from a whole array of foreign clubs.

Amongst them were Barcelona, who would soon tempt Everton to accept a £2.7m offer that brought to an end a brief, yet action-packed Goodison career for the man with the golden boots.

Lineker had struggled to impress the Evertonians early on, but once the goals started to flow, they very quickly began to appreciate his special qualities in front of goal.

As the season drew to a close, he was attempting to become only the second Goodison player since the war to score 30 League goals.

He needed two against West Ham to match Bob Latchford's 1977-78 feat and got off the mark after 43 minutes, lashing home from close range after Paul Wilkinson had knocked on a Gary Stevens free-kick.

Kevin Sheedy almost broke the cross bar at the Stanley Park End with a thundering effort on the stroke of half-

time. And three minutes into the second half, Lineker pounced on a Stewart error to clip his second goal past the advancing Parkes.

The Hammers were on the rack and Wilkinson sent a header against the post before forcing Stewart to concede a penalty. Lineker had the opportunity to take it and claim his hat-trick.

A third League goal would have seen him equal the 31 goals scored by John Willie Parker for Everton in the

Gary Lineker had one memorable goalscoring season at Goodison Park, finishing with 40 goals. He is seen here in acrobatic action against Nottingham Forest in August 1989.

The fences came down at Goodison in April 1989, 11 years after they were erected. This followed immediately after the Hillsborough Disaster which claimed the lives of 95 Liverpudlians.

1953-54 Second Division season. But Lineker shunned the opportunity to bag his second treble in three days to allow Trevor Steven to slot home from the spot and make it 3-0.

West Ham's consolation goal came in the final minute, scored by a player who would eventually be signed by the Blues — Tony Cottee. But the applause on the final whistle was very much for Lineker & Co as they looked forward to their Wembley confrontation with the old enemy. Sadly, Gary had glittered for the last time at Goodison.

Everton: Mimms; Stevens, Van Den Hauwe, Ratcliffe, Billing, Richardson, Steven, Lineker(Aspinall), Wilkinson, Heath, Sheedy.

An aerial shot of Goodison in October 1986, looking towards the Gwladys Street End. The famous terraces are clearly visible. The land cleared behind the Gwladys Street Stand is now occupied by new houses.

Factfile: Everton's decision to sell Lineker, a man who had scored 40 goals in total for the Blues, caused some controversy, to say the least. But manager Howard Kendall's decision proved justified the following season when the Blues regained the Championship they had lost to Liverpool. The scoring load was spread around instead of being dominated by one man. And yet the debate about the sale of Lineker inevitably continues, simply because in recent years he has remained a goalscorer with few equals. But managers cannot concern themselves with what might have been. It's enough to say that the England star was given a top-class stage at Goodison Park, a ground he still regards as one of his favourite venues.

The first of two Trevor Steven penalty successes against Luton Town as the Champions celebrate with a 3-1 win.

Two Title Trophies In One Day!

Saturday, 9 May 1987

Everton 3 Luton Town 1

THE sun shone on Goodison Park to welcome home the newly-crowned League Champions. Luton Town provided the opposition for this final game of the 1987 season, but it was not so much a football match as a carnival.

Five days earlier, amidst incredible scenes of jubilation at Carrow Road, Everton had stormed to a title-clinching victory over Norwich City, courtesy of an unlikely goal hero, Pat Van Den Hauwe.

He was an intimidating full-back who bristled and battled his way through matches with a fierce glare that put the fear of God into opponents. At Norwich,

he suddenly took on a new persona. It was the day that 'Psycho Pat' picked up a new nickname — Pat Van Den Howitzer!

Having struggled for 90 minutes to turn the Championship screw against Manchester City, the Blues took just 45 seconds to produce the goods against shell-shocked Norwich.

A cracking effort, straight out of the Kevin Sheedy shooting manual, exploded from the right boot of a man who was more renowned for his ferocious tackling.

The 7,000 Evertonians who had made the long trek to East Anglia, let out a deafening roar. It was only matched by the scenes of unbridled joy and elation at Goodison when Luton came to town, bit players in a Champion production.

Trevor Steven is bundled off the ball against Luton, but he had the last laugh, scoring from the resulting penalty.

It began with Kevin Ratcliffe leading his teammates out to collect not one, but two title trophies. The Football League had been sponsored by the 'Today' newspaper and their award was soon being passed between the delighted Everton players while skipper Ratcliffe paraded the more familiar and historic League Championship trophy.

Flags and banners were waved and there was even a mini tickertape reception. A special cheer was reserved for injured right-back Paul Power.

But would Luton play ball and give the new Champions an easy ride? It

Factfile: Everton's celebrating fans were soon caught up in a management sensation when Howard Kendall decided to accept a Continental challange with Spanish club Athletic Bilbao. The board had no hesitation in handing the vacant Goodison hot-seat to Kendall's highly respected assistant Colin Harvey.

became clear that they had not read the script when Mark Stein blasted them into the lead with a fierce shot. Inspired by the combative Peter Reid, Everton now swept forward, virtually camping inside their opponents' half. It all went wrong for the visitors just before the break.

Goalkeeper Les Sealey took a kick in the face from Graeme Sharp and was concussed. For a tense moment, there were fears that he had swallowed his tongue and was struggling to breathe, but after a lengthy delay the 'keeper climbed to his feet to warm applause and resumed between the posts.

Sealey was not the happiest man in the ground at that moment in time and his frustration bubbled over in the 52nd minute when Everton secured a deserved equaliser. Reid showed great skill, beating two men on the edge of the box before chipping in a ball that came back off the bar.

Johnson handled in the melee that followed, Sealey showing his anger at the penalty decision by hurling the ball

215

Thanks fans . . .skipper Kevin Ratcliffe leads the applause as the 1987 Champions bask in the glory at Goodison after the Luton game.

towards the referee. Trevor Steven retained his composure, slotting home his shot before the 'keeper was booked for booting the ball away.

Minutes later Steven repeated the act after he had been fouled by North. All hopes the Hatters had of salvaging a point disappeared when Nicholas was sent off after tangling with Reid.

The carnival had turned into something much more combative, but Everton provided the perfect finale when Sharp turned in Gary Stevens' drive to illustrate the Blues' superiority and make it 3-1.

After the match, the trophy-laden Ratcliffe led the players on a lap of honour to the euphoric chant of "Champions, Champions". As manager Howard Kendall and coach Colin Harvey watched from the sidelines, no one in the ground could have envisaged the upheaval that would soon follow. But for now it was a case of soaking up the glory and enjoying every single second.
Everton Southall; Stevens, Watson, Ratcliffe, Van Den Hauwe, Steven, Snodin, Reid, Harper, Heath, Sharp. Substitute: Adams.

Peter Beardsley opened the scoring for Liverpool, the first of eight goals on a remarkable Goodison Cup night. Beardsley, of course, is now a committed Evertonian.

The Match Of A Lifetime

Wednesday, 20 February 1991

Everton 4 Liverpool 4

THIS FA Cup fifth-round replay between soccer's greatest rivals was to turn into a remarkable three-match marathon that included a clash, described by all those lucky enough to see it, as the 'Game of a lifetime!'

Senior fans would still argue that the 1935 FA Cup replay against Sunderland, a 6-4 bonanza in the Blues' favour, was the greatest Goodison encounter of all time.

But this modern Cup classic surely rivalled it for sensational goals and breathtaking action. And the fact that it was a 'derby' game of epic proportions added to the magic of the 1991 battle.

It will also be remembered as Kenny Dalglish's Liverpool swansong. Within days, he had resigned his position as manager in the most sensational of circumstances, claiming he could not cope with the intense pressure of being in one of the hottest seats in the business.

It meant that the Reds had to go into the second replay with a caretaker boss in the shape of that old Anfield veteran Ronnie Moran. Everton would win a

nail-biting Goodison tie 1-0, but at times it was the soccer equivalent of Custer's Last Stand!

When the teams first came out of the hat together, no one could possibly have envisaged the drama that lay ahead. The first game, played at Anfield, was controversial enough. Howard Kendall and Colin Harvey plotted an audacious coup that might have come off if referee Neil Midgley had not denied the Blues what appeared to be a clear penalty.

Gary Ablett, ironically a man who would join Everton the following season, pole-axed Pat Nevin as the winger broke into the right of the box. Not only did Midgley refuse the spot-kick appeals, he made it patently clear that if Nevin 'dived' again, he would be sent off.

The Evertonians, not surprisingly, were furious. The match finished up 0-0, but that incident served to fire up the Blues for the replay.

The same official was in charge at Goodison Park. When he emerged prior to the kick-off to be photographed receiving the official match ball, a home fan leapt forward and put a red scarf around his neck. The experienced Bolton referee, a man with quite a

Graeme Sharp
pounces to score his
first goal on a night
of Cup passion.

Graeme Sharp's
second strike had
Steve Nicol
grounded and in
trouble.

reputation for his after-dinner speeches, saw the funny side and almost certainly used it at his next speaking engagement.

In the meantime, he concentrated his thoughts on this cup return, Dalglish inspiring the Liverpudlians by naming Peter Beardsley up front alongside Ian Rush. There had been much controversy across the park about the manager's apparent reluctance to give the Geordie star a regular place, even though he was a firm favourite with the fans.

This would eventually culminate in Beardsley accepting a surprise offer from

Howard Kendall to join Everton. But for now, he was very much a Kop idol.

And he had the visiting fans on their feet after just three minutes with a swerving drive that was parried by Neville Southall, the goalkeeper recovering to snatch the ball away from the marauding Rush.

Liverpool finally went in front after 32 minutes when Kevin Ratcliffe was dispossessed by Rush, who sped goalwards to draw Southall and shoot towards an unguarded net. Incredibly, defender Andy Hinchcliffe cleared off

Sharp turns away to celebrate with his fellow Scot, Pat Nevin, in an amazing FA Cup replay.

Delighted substitute
Tony Cottee gets on
the scoreboard to
stun Liverpool.

the line, only for the alert Rush to nod the loose ball to Beardsley who scored.

The Reds continued to hold sway with Jan Molby lording it in centre midfield. Now Kendall replaced the unhappy Ray Atteveld with Stuart McCall and two minutes after the interval, Everton equalised. Hinchcliffe curled in a left-wing cross and Graeme Sharp arrived to power in a header which Bruce Grobbelaar could only push on to the inside of the post, the ground erupting as the ball found the back of the net.

The Blues now took control with Sharp ready to fight for every ball and every situation. Nevin scooped over and Mike Newell volleyed wide, only for Beardsley to respond with a cracking left-foot shot after 71 minutes that restored his side's lead.

But no sooner had the visiting cheers died away, when Sharp lifted Everton's spirits with a vital equaliser following a misunderstanding between Grobbelaar and Steve Nicol. Liverpool now demonstrated their Champion spirit by going ahead for the third time after 77 minutes, when Molby's cross was nodded home by Rush.

Few people in the ground thought

Everton would recover from this body blow, but their resilience on the night was quite remarkble. Only 60 seconds were remaining when Tony Cottee, an 85th-minute replacement for Nevin, raced on to McCall's pass to score a

Factfile: Everton lived extremely dangerously in the third encounter, played at Goodison after the Blues won the toss for venue. They managed to take the lead for the first time in 222 minutes of Cup football when centre-back Dave Watson cashed in after a moment of panic in the Liverpool area.

The game was 12 minutes old when an Atteveld free-kick was flicked on, first by Sharp and then by Watson. Nicol tried to clear, but he could only glance the ball backwards and Martin Keown was able to get in a shot that Grobbelaar saved with an outstretched boot. The ball dropped at Molby's feet and the Dane somehow allowed it to squirm through his legs. A grateful Watson hammered it home from close range and Everton would now dig in to claim victory.

clinical equaliser that forced the tie into extra-time.

At this stage, the fans were as exhausted as the players. Liverpool went for the early knockout blow in the extra period, but the superb Southall claimed a cross-shot from Barnes, a Rush header and a point-blank range effort from Barry Venison.

But even the famous Welsh international 'keeper had no chance when Barnes curled home a superb right-foot shot from the edge of the box after 102 minutes.

It meant Liverpool were in front for the fourth time. It was all or nothing for Everton and they came up trumps with Cottee proving a real 'super sub'. With six minutes left, he fired in a shot that found the net through Grobbelaar's legs after Glenn Hysen had allowed Molby's attempted backpass to run on into the box.

It was 4-4 and when Midgley finally called an end, both teams received a memorable standing ovation. The only snag was, they had to go through it all again the following Wednesday. Could the players and the supporters last the pace? This was now the million-dollar question.

Everton: Southall; Atteveld (McCall 46), Watson, Keown, Ratcliffe, Hinchcliffe, Nevin (Cottee 85), McDonald, Ebbrell, Sharp, Newell.

Cottee plunders his second and Everton's fourth as a remarkable game reaches its climax.

It's 4-4 . . .and Liverpool goalkeeper Bruce Grobbelaar just cannot believe it.

Tony Cottee scores the only goal of the game against Luton and the Gwladys Street fans, standing for the last time, cheer on an afternoon of mixed emotions.

Gwladys Street's Last Stand

Saturday, 4 May 1991

Everton 1 Luton Town 0

THIS was the day when I put my reporter's notebook to one side, turned my back on the Press Box and joined the faithful on the Gwladys Street terraces for an afternoon of nostalgia.

It was the day supporters stood on that famous bank of terracing for the very last time prior to seats being installed. As a kid, I'd been a fully paid-up member of this section, first cheering on Dave Hickson and later saluting the likes of Bobby Collins, Roy Vernon, Alex Young and the rest.

It was the first time I had stood on the Gwladys Street for over 20 years, but it was fascinating to climb on to the famous shelf, that slightly elevated section of terracing, to reclaim my old 'spec' in the company of my own two boys, Colin and Peter.

Maybe you look back on things through rose-tinted glasses, but I seemed to remember the support being that much more raucous and passionate. But it wasn't the greatest of games and the supporters ran hot and cold.

The sun came out and things began to look up with Robert Warzycha and Tony Cottee playing their part. It was Cottee who scored the only goal of the game, seizing control after Stuart McCall had blocked an attempted clearance.

Cottee rounded 'keeper Alec Chamberlain and gleefully slotted home his 22nd goal of the season.

It was enough to secure victory, but here was a day when the result was irrelevant. The old ground would never quite be the same again for those supporters as they wended their way away from the Gwladys Street terraces. It was now just a part of Goodison folklore.

Everton: Southall; Ebbrell, Hinchliffe, Ratcliffe, Watson, Atteveld, Warzycha, McCall, Newell, Cottee, Beagrie.
Attendance: 19,909

Opposite page: Gwladys Street's last stand . . .the end of an era at Goodison Park as the home fans stand for the last time.

The crash barriers are removed in readiness for seats installed in May 1991.

The new Gwladys Street roof began to take shape in the summer of 1987.

Enter Peter Beardsley — The Geordie Genius

Saturday, 21 September 1991

Everton 3 Coventry City 0

THE summer of 1991 was a tricky one for Everton manager Howard Kendall. He had pursued Derby County striker Dean Saunders for months, only to be disappointed at the last possible moment when the Welsh international chose to sign for arch-rivals Liverpool.

But this was not to be the end of the story. Saunders' arrival at Anfield marked the beginning of the end for Kop favourite Peter Beardsley. One of the game's great entertainers inexplicably found himself struggling to nail down a regular place in season 1990-91.

Kendall, seeing his chance, offered Liverpool £1m for a player who had been a thorn in Everton's side on more than one occasion in derby battles. Graeme Souness, having invested over £4m on Saunders and his Baseball Ground teammate Mark Wright, decided to accept the bid and one of the most remarkable deals of recent years was completed with the Blues' boss delighted to have captured such a class act.

There were those at Anfield who thought Beardsley would not have the 'bottle' to maintain his high level of performance across the park and that the transfer, at such a late stage in his career, might backfire on the talented Geordie. He would soon prove that there is no substitute for star quality.

Beardsley demonstrated clearly that it's not the colour of the shirt that is important, but rather the ability and character of the man wearing it. The Evertonians took to him from the moment he made his League debut against Nottingham Forest on 17 August, 1991.

The campaign itself would prove

highly frustrating for the Blues. They began so brightly, showing skill and flair to earn special salutes from a host of rival managers, not least Brian Clough (Forest), Alex Ferguson (Manchester United) and Dave Stringer (Norwich). But as the year progressed, Everton somehow lost their way.

It was left to Beardsley — backed up by men like Dave Watson and Martin Keown — to try and keep the fans smiling through a difficult spell.

The Geordie star would finish with 20 goals, his First Division return proving superior to Saunders, the man who replaced him at Anfield. This, in itself, had to be a source of satisfaction to the Evertonians.

One of the highlights was Beardsley's Goodison Park hat-trick against Coventry City. There was an element of good fortune about the first goal, scored after 40 minutes. Former Everton defender Brian Borrows, in attempting to clear a Mike Newell cross, succeeded only in playing the ball against the legs of the in-running Beardsley. The ball richochetted towards the corner of the net and while goalkeeper Steve Ogrizovic got a hand to it, he couldn't prevent a goal.

But there was certainly nothing lucky about the Geordie's second after 61 minutes. Robert Warzycha's testing cross was only half cleared and Beardsley crashed it home with venom from the edge of the box. Manager Kendall later suggested it was exactly the kind of goal the player used to score on derby day . . .against the Blues!

The hat-trick was completed 15 minutes from time. Neil McDonald, a second-half subsitute for Kevin Sheedy, sent Mark Ward racing into the box. He appeared to be fouled by the luckless Borrows, but the referee intially ignored the spot-kick appeals. It was only when he spotted a linesman's flag did he finally stop play.

Beardsley, completely unruffled by the Coventry complaints, stepped up to fire the penalty hard and low into the bottom corner. The home fans celebrated with a chant that would echo around Goodison Park all season: "There's only one Peter Beardsley!"

Everton: Southall; Atteveld, Hinchcliffe, Ebbrell, Watson, Keown, Warzycha, Beardsley, Newell, Sheedy (McDonald), Ward. Substitute: Cottee. *Attendance: 20,542*

Peter Beardsley celebrates with his teammates after scoring against Crystal Palace.

226

Farewell to 1991-2.
Peter Beardsley and
Neville Southall
salute the fans after
the final game
against Chelsea.

Servants Of Everton

DOWN the years, Everton have been lucky enough to have men of rare dedication guiding their fortunes. George Mahon, the Goodison Park visionary, has been given much prominence along with Dr James Clement Baxter, who held the record for official service until his death in 1928. Dr Baxter, whose generosity eased the club's financial worries during those early months at Goodison in 1892, clocked up 39 years service on the board, many of them as chairman.

In 1895, following a major board upheaval, the name of Mr Will Cuff came to the fore. He would become a Goodison Park marathon man, exerting his strong will on the club until he resigned from the board in May 1948

228

after an internal wrangle with fellow directors.

Cuff had links with the St Domingo Church from which Everton emanated. He became an Everton member in 1890 and supported the club through the difficult times of 1892 when the move from Anfield to Goodison was completed. In 1901, he stepped down from the board to become club secretary, succeeding Mr Richard Molyneux.

He held this office until 1918, when he resigned because it was affecting his work as a solicitor (his Everton work was unpaid). But Cuff returned to the board in 1921, became chairman a year later and retained that high office until 1938. He continued as a director for a further ten years. It meant that, apart from his three year break, he had powerful connections with the Blues for over half a century.

Cuff also worked tirelessly for the Football League, becoming president in 1940. He joined the Management Committee in 1925, taking 42 out of a possible 43 votes. In 1929, he sucessfully campaigned for the automatic election of Management Committee members on to the FA Council. On the home front,

In November 1934, Everton vice-chairman Mr Ernest Green received a gold wristlet watch from chairman Mr W.C.Cuff to mark his 21 years service. To Mr Cuff's right (arms folded) is former player Jack Sharp, who by now was a director. Second from right is Dr C.Baxter (son of Goodison pioneer Dr J.C.Baxter).

he was at the helm as Everton suffered relegation for the first time, bounced back to gain promotion, won the League Championship and then the FA Cup.

Dixie Dean called him 'The Master'. One or two of his rivals called him other things. Cuff was a man who did not sit on the fence and he was never scared to ruffle feathers. He was largely responsible for selling Everton's original training ground to a brewery for £60,000 and then buying the present Bellefield site in West Derby from the Co-op for £30,000.

Much earlier, in 1911, he had realised the importance of having a strong supplementary League to bring players through and give experienced players out of favour the opportunity to retain their match fitness. Hence, the Central League was born which is still going strong today, containing the reserve teams of many of the top clubs, including Everton.

As League president, he handled the sometimes bitter negotiations with the Players' Union over wages. He got players' shirts numbered, helped to introduce the transfer system and then fought hard, but without success, to limit the fees which he felt were getting totally out of hand. He helped to devise the offside law and the methods of promotion and relegation. In other words, he was a man who got things done.

But in his later years, Cuff began to fall out with his fellow Everton directors. Some of them accused him of

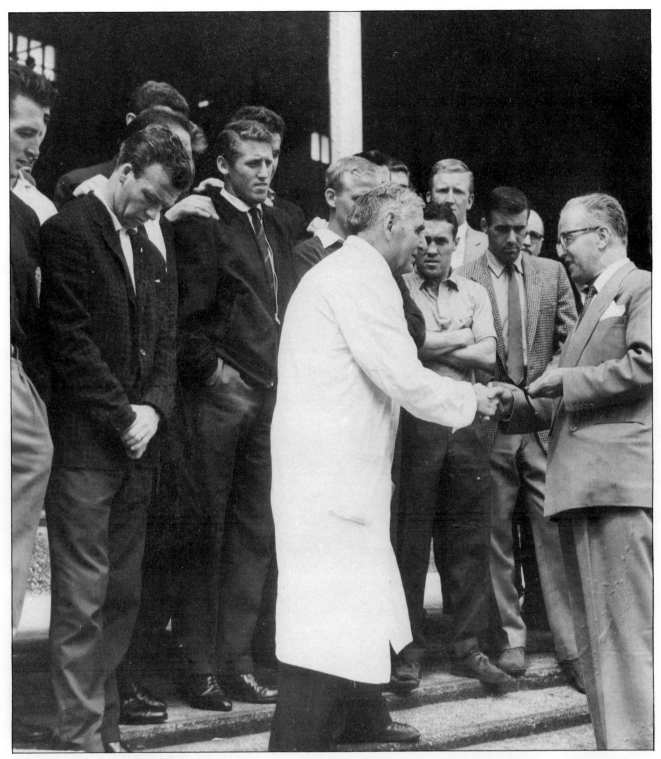

wrongful use of proxy votes at a shareholders' meeting. He denied this totally. They also complained that he was critical of club policy, or as he called it, lack of policy. The man himself, now 76, felt his vast experience gave him the right to express his opinions, even if contrary to the views of fellow directors.

There was an uneasy peace for three years, intermingled with spells of bitterness, before Cuff finally resigned in May 1948. He died soon after, on 6 February 1949. His epitaph was not as a trouble-maker, but as a trouble-shooter, a real leader of men, and most of all a dedicated Evertonian.

He was the loudest and most influential voice Everton have ever had on the Football League Management Committee. It's worth charting other Goodison 'League' men:

R.Molyneux served the Management Committee 1893-95; Dr.J.C.Baxter 1904-19; Cuff 1925-36, also being vice-president 1936-39, president 1939-49 and

It's the end of a Goodison Park era. Everton chairman John Moores presents a gold wristlet watch to Harry Cooke on 28 July 1961 to mark the famous old trainer's retirement after 58 years service to the club. The Cooke link continued when grandson Harry Cooke became chief scout.

life member 1945-49; P.D.Carter was president from 1986-89. Sir Philip Carter, of course, remains an Everton board member, having been chairman through the most successful spell in the club's history when the League Championship (twice), FA Cup and European Cup-winners' Cup came to Goodison Park in the 1980s.

The present members of the Everton

Everton's chairman throughout the most successful period in the club's history was Philip Carter (now Sir Philip), who is pictured in August 1981 in one of Goodison's impressive Executive Boxes. His loyalty to manager Howard Kendall would pay off handsomely as the 1980s progressed.

board in this, Goodison Park's Centenary year, are: Dr David M.Marsh (chairman), Desmond Pitcher (deputy chairman), Alan Waterworth, Keith Tamlin, Sir Philip Carter, David Newton, Bill Kenwright. Secretary and chief executive as the Blues head into a bold new era in the newly-formed Premier League is Jim Greenwood.

The Gwladys Street End were convinced that Liverpool's Bruce Grobbelaar was a clown and so a couple of Goodison jesters decided to keep the Liverpool 'keeper company during the derby clash of March, 1982. Bruce saw the funny side and had the last laugh. Everton lost 3-1.

The old clock at the Gwladys Street End, long since gone, offered an unusual, if somewhat dangerous vantage point for this young fan when Manchester United were the visitors in December 1975. He saw Bob Latchford score in a 1-1 draw.

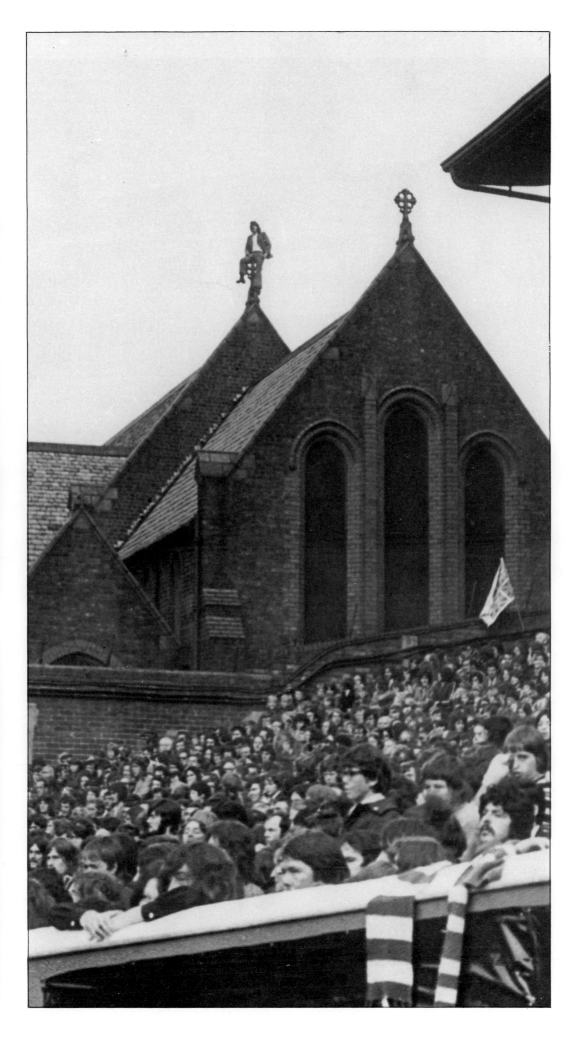

Evertonians have gone to remarkable lengths to watch their team down the years. In 1973, one fan took up a precarious position on the church roof at the Gwladys Street End.

The other Goodison Park! Everton daft Harold Boswell painted his Birkenhead house blue and white in 1977 and named it after his favourite ground. It included the club crest, pennants, posters and a flag run up the nearest lamp post. While his wife Lynne was still in hospital after having a baby son, Harold nipped off to register the birth, naming the boy after the entire Everton team. A furious mum stuck to her original choice – Jason.